WATERSIDE
In Nottinghamshire

G000275738

Peter Fooks

COUNTRYSIDE BOOKS
NEWBURY, BERKSHIRE

COUNTRYSIDE BOOKS
3 Catherine Road
Newbury, Berkshire

ISBN 1 85306 559 5

Designed by Graham Whiteman
Cover illustration by Colin Doggett
Maps and photographs by the author

Produced through MRM Associates Ltd., Reading
Printed by J. W. Arrowsmith Ltd., Bristol

Contents

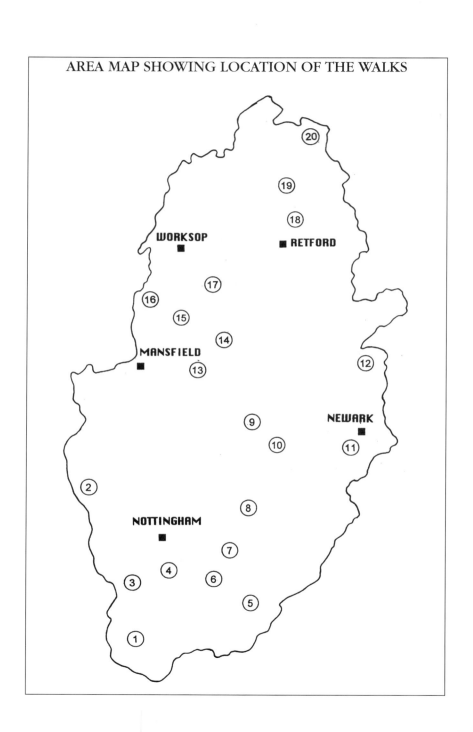

AREA MAP SHOWING LOCATION OF THE WALKS

Walk

PUBLISHER'S NOTE

We hope that you obtain considerable enjoyment from this book; great care has been taken in its preparation. Although at the time of publication all routes followed public rights of way or permitted paths, diversion orders can be made and permissions withdrawn.

We cannot of course be held responsible for such diversion orders and any inaccuracies in the text which result from these or any changes to the routes nor any damage which might result from walkers trespassing on private property. We are anxious though that all details covering the walks are kept up to date and would therefore welcome information from readers which would be relevant to future editions.

INTRODUCTION

It is many years since I caught my first tiddler in the Trent. In those bare-knee days, my knowledge of Nottinghamshire's waterways was confined to the Trent, the Leen, the Soar – and Grantham Canal. I was never a great angler. Wriggling maggots never did anything for me, and I could never face, with equanimity, the prospect of having to remove a struggling roach or perch from my hook. A gudgeon in a jam-jar was my limit. But, since those early days with garden cane and bent pin, I have become familiar with many of our local waters. I have swum in the Trent, picnicked by the Soar, rowed on Highfields Lake, camped by the Maun and the Smite. Even skated on the floodlands.

Nowadays, without a great deal of thought, I could jot down the names of more than a dozen rivers, about half a dozen canals, and innumerable brooks, becks and dumbles. Not to mention a host of man-made water features – lakes, ponds and pools – many of which have been adapted from worked out gravel pits and the like, and which now make a genuine and attractive contribution to our recreational heritage. Nottinghamshire is not lacking in attractive waterways.

This book of walks is intended to introduce the reader to some of our most enticing Nottinghamshire waterway features. Not all of them, because there are still a few areas that, for one reason or another – lack of suitable rights of way, or absence of adequate refreshment facilities, for instance – defied my best efforts.

Our principal river is, of course, the Trent, which flows for some 70 miles – from the south-west of the county to the extreme north-east. An interesting side-effect is that every other river, brook or feature included here falls within the same catchment area, and thus has a direct affinity with the Trent, as a tributary or otherwise. I have made use of this fact in assembling the walks, using the downstream flow of the Trent as my base-line, starting in the south-west of the county, on the River Soar and the Kingston Brook, and finishing in the extreme north-east, where the tidal Trent finally leaves the county.

The walks vary in length between 2 and 7 miles; all have been checked in detail and none should present any problems, other than those posed by climate and the seasonal demands of agriculture. A number can be followed – or adapted for use – by wheelchair users (see Walks 2, 3, 4, 18 and 19). The sketch maps provided are for general guidance only, and should not be regarded as definitive. You are recommended to use the correct OS maps as listed in the walk details.

Every walk includes some form of refreshment stop; either a pub or a good tea-room. Whether or not you use them is, of course, up to you. If you prefer to picnic, be sure to abide by the country code, and take your litter home. Wherever you park your car, do so with common-sense and courtesy. Do not block anyone's entrance – and that includes farm gates. If using the listed pubs or tea-rooms, always obtain permission before leaving your transport there. For non-drivers, I have provided basic details of public transport, together with telephone contact numbers. There are also suggested places of interest nearby, to make the most of your day out.

One last thing: always observe the Country Code, remembering that the countryside where you walk is somebody else's home and/or workshop. In particular – because I have had occasion to clear up after a particularly loutish set of visitors – do not leave litter, such as empty beer cans and plastic bottles. If they are light enough to carry when they are full, they will not be too heavy when they are empty!

Happy walking!

Peter Fooks

ALONG THE KINGSTON BROOK

One of the most attractive features of Nottinghamshire's south-west corner is the River Soar, which shadows the county boundary from Stanford, near Loughborough, to the River Trent. For much of the way, a popular footpath follows the riverside meadows, with rivercraft and wildfowl in plenty to delight the eye. The Kingston Brook enters the Soar near Kingston village and both waterways enhance this walk to three attractive villages.

The 'Old Cut', near Kegworth.

In one of the quieter corners of the county, the villages of West Leake and Kingston on Soar are two of our prettiest and least spoilt settlements. Although only a small village, West Leake is not without historical interest. The little 12th century village church contains, among other features, three interesting medieval monuments, and a more recent window depicting a charming view of the church itself and the local scene. Lord Belper, of nearby Kingston, who used to own West Leake, provided the village school – now serving as the village hall

– in 1850. Traditionally, the principal local industry has been farming, but an interesting variation was osier growing. This led to the establishment here of a flourishing basket-making industry, which in turn spread to neighbouring villages. The founder's home incorporated, as well as the basket-making facility, an inn and the village oven. Kingston on Soar has an aura of peace, with its pretty village green and ancient cottages. The village's name prompts an intriguing speculation: when the villagers of neighbouring Gotham 'persuaded' King John to by-pass their village, did he build his lodge, instead, at 'Kingston'? The third village on this walk – Sutton Bonington – though somewhat larger, is equally attractive, and has a particular importance of its own. It is the home of Nottingham University's School of Agriculture, founded in 1895 as the Midland Dairy Institute; a fact emphasised by the tidiness of the fields hereabouts – and by the well-maintained condition of the footpaths! The delightful River Soar is close at hand, and bearing in mind the quiet, rural nature of the district, it is easy to forget that the East Midlands Airport and the M1 motorway are so easily accessible.

The Star inn is just outside the village of West Leake, and can be heartily recommended as a refreshment stop, before or after the walk. We are told there used to be a cock pit here, in less compassionate times, explaining the pub's alternative local name of 'The Leake Pit House'. The Star – an Enterprise Inns house – has been an inn since about 1750, and has a charming old-world atmosphere. Food is available daily at lunchtime, and also in the evening from Tuesday to Saturday. The lunchtime fare on Monday is restricted to filled rolls and ploughman's lunches. At other times, the menu varies from day to day, with a selection of home-cooked dishes, salads, curries and fish to whet the appetite. Speciality ales include Bass and various guest beers. Families are welcome, and there is a popular children's play area and an attractive beer garden.

Telephone: 01509 852233.

● **HOW TO GET THERE:** Follow the A453 (M1 Link) from Nottingham to Ratcliffe on Soar power station, turning off south here to reach West Leake. In the village, turn right and follow the road round to the next junction, and the Star inn. Alternatively, West Leake can be reached via the A60 (Nottingham-Loughborough road), turning off, west, at Costock crossroads and right again by East Leake church.

The only bus service to West Leake is an occasional Soar Valley

Community bus, Monday to Saturday. Sutton Bonington (from where the walk can be started) is better served, by Barton's route 10 (Monday to Saturday, hourly) or Barton's/Nottingham City Transport route 310 (Sunday, three-hourly).

- **PARKING:** If visiting the Star, you may park there, subject to the licensee's permission. Alternatively, there is a large lay-by area a few hundred yards along Melton Lane, to the west of the pub.
- **LENGTH OF THE WALK:** 6 miles. Maps: OS Landranger 129 Nottingham and Loughborough, OS Pathfinder 853 Loughborough North (GR 524261).

THE WALK

1. Starting from the Star, follow the side lane back towards West Leake, crossing the Kingston Brook and turning left on the bend at the west end of the village. Follow the waymarked lane (RUPP) west, into open country. Keep to the lane, bending right and left at Scotland Farm. Bear left then on the waymarked bridleway, and pass to the left of a large pond. Continue to a bridge over the Kingston Brook.

2. Turn right, following the brook and the hedge round to a stile. Cross, and rejoin the brook, crossing the footbridge and turning right. Keep to the brookside path, passing Kingston Hall visible across the stream. It is the family home of Lord Belper, a descendant of the hosiery manufacturer Jedediah Strutt. Bear left in the last field to cross a stile and reach the road, just outside Kingston on Soar village.

3. The footpath continues over the road, crossing a stile and turning left as directed by the guidepost. Cross a farm lane to the left of farm buildings, passing to the left of a silage clamp and continuing over the fields. Pass under the railway via the footpath bridge and straight ahead to the road. Turn left.

4. On the bend by Kegworth Bridge, keep straight forward over the stile and join the riverside (River Soar) path. Follow the river and the 'Old Cut', passing Kegworth Deep Lock, and continue. Just prior to a mooring area (on the right bank) turn left and follow Soar Lane to Sutton Bonington. The village was formerly two hamlets, Sutton and Bonington. The local economy was traditionally based on agriculture and framework knitting, and in the 19th century there were as many as 50 stockingers' workshops here. One of the most noteworthy buildings

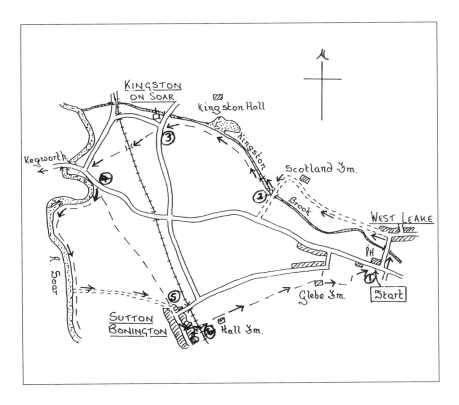

in the village is, perhaps, 'Hobgoblins'. This late 17th century (or thereabouts) large stone house is reputed to be haunted and – rather less likely – to have a secret tunnel leading to St Anne's church.

5. Keep straight forward along Main Street, towards the parish church. Turn left at Bollards Lane, passing the Anchor Inn. The road fades to a track between houses and has all the appearance of a private drive. But this is the correct route and, after bending right with the track, a footpath will be seen bearing away on your left. Follow this, and cross the railway.

6. Continue along the enclosed footpath to Hall Farm. Pass the farm on its left and keep on ahead, with the hedge on your right. Follow the waymarked route around Glebe Farm, returning to the hedge-side and continuing for the length of one field, then left along its width. Turn right and left through the hedges and bear right to cross the remaining fields, back to your starting point.

Crossing Kingston Brook.

PLACES OF INTEREST

The *Great Central Railway* at Loughborough Central Station offers the experience of main line expresses, on 8 miles of track, hauled by steam locos. Trains run at weekends throughout the year and daily in high season. Sunday lunch and afternoon tea can be enjoyed during the journey. For confirmation of opening times and fares, ring 01509 230726. Also in Loughborough, the *John Taylor Bell Museum* provides a fascinating and educational display, set in the world's largest bell foundry complex. Open Tuesday to Saturday and Bank Holidays. Telephone 01509 233414.

THE BEAUTY OF THE EREWASH VALLEY

The River Soar meets the Trent below Red Hill, on the county boundary with Leicestershire and Derbyshire. In the same area, but from the north, the River Erewash and the Erewash Canal also join the Trent. Surprising beauty can be found in the most unlikely of places, as you will discover on this canal-side walk made fascinating by wild life and a colourful living waterway.

The Great Northern Basin.

There are pockets of real charm here, though the border towns of Ilkeston, Heanor, Eastwood and Langley Mill could not be described as popular tourist areas! Long blighted by the effects of industries such as coal mining, textiles and ironworks, it might be supposed that nothing of beauty remained hereabouts. But that would be a false assumption, and nowhere more so than along the line of the Erewash Canal. This area was beloved of the author D.H.Lawrence, who lived close by here

13

at Eastwood and whose father worked at the nearby Brinsley Colliery. The Erewash Canal was built 1777/9 to provide easy transport from the coalfields. Nearly 12 miles long, the canal extends from Langley Mill to Trent Lock. The Nottingham Canal was constructed between 1792 and 1796 to compete with the Erewash Canal, and follows a roughly parallel course as far as Trowell, where it swings east. The total length is nearly 15 miles, of which about half still survives. The two halves of the walk are entirely different. On the outward journey through the Nottingham Canal Nature Reserve, the line of the canal is followed but this is largely dry or heavily overgrown with reeds and other flora, and is a haven for wildlife, particularly mallard. The return journey follows the Erewash Canal, features being the two locks (Shipley Gate and Eastwood), the Great Northern Basin, and the life (boats and wildfowl) of the canal.

The Great Northern at Langley Mill is an attractive, traditional English pub, with a welcoming ambience and obliging management and staff. The house fronts onto the busy A608 road, but a secluded angle of the outside area overlooks the Great Northern Basin where once the Cromford Canal gave way to the twin Nottingham and Erewash Canals, making it a pleasant place to stop at when beginning or ending the walk. There is a full range of meals on offer here, with a choice of fish or poultry dishes, pies, salads or grills, and a mouth-watering selection of snacks and sandwiches. Vegetarians and children are catered for, and a Senior Citizen's Special is available every Wednesday lunchtime at a 20% discount.

Telephone: 01773 712804.

- **HOW TO GET THERE:** Eastwood and Langley Mill lie on the A608 (Derby/Mansfield) road, on either side of the A610 (Nottingham/ Ripley). The walk starts from the Great Northern inn, immediately adjacent to the road junction, on its western side.

  The area is well served with buses from surrounding towns: Nottingham, Derby, Mansfield, Sutton, Heanor etc.
- **PARKING:** Roadside parking space is available on the side roads adjacent to the Great Northern although in the week this tends to be heavily used by workers from the industrial estate. Alternative space is available adjacent to the Nottingham Canal Nature Reserve, at the head of Anchor Road, and it is advisable to follow the route from here, thus avoiding the difficult A608 road crossing, if accompanied by wheelchair users.

- **LENGTH OF THE WALK:** 3 miles (2½ miles from Anchor Road). Maps: OS Landranger 129 Nottingham and Loughborough, OS Pathfinder 812 Nottingham North & Ilkeston (GR 455471).

THE WALK

1. From the Great Northern, cross the main road – with care – and follow Anchor Road. This metalled country lane runs parallel to the A610, but is shielded from it by a line of tall trees.

2. Turn the bend by the Anchor Road parking area (starting point for the shortened walk) and join the waymarked footpath following the line of the Nottingham Canal. It is dry here, but some elements of the

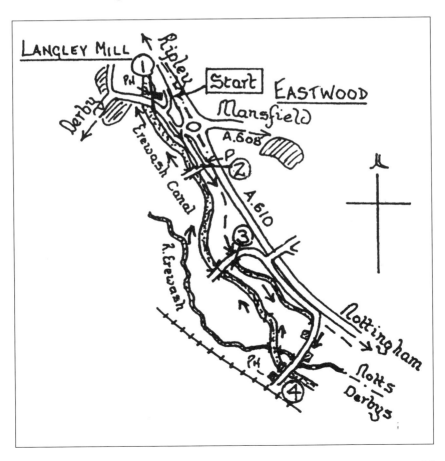

The Erewash Canal.

canal can still be found, much of it overgrown and forming a delightful nature trail, as you proceed. The waterway visible to the right, in the early stages, is the Erewash Canal, which you will be following on the return leg of your journey.

3. On meeting a rough track, turn right over the bridge and then left again, still following the line of the canal as far as the next junction; a metalled road. Turn right, and descend the hill to Shipley Lock, on the Erewash Canal. Unlike the Nottingham Canal, much of which has been obliterated by opencast working and redevelopment and in other parts allowed to revert to nature, the Erewash Canal has been maintained and restored as a living waterway, with working locks, colourful narrow boats, anglers and waterfowl. The canal follows the county boundary, although traditionally one canal was in Derbyshire and the other in Nottinghamshire – competing for trade. It might be argued that the Erewash puts the Nottingham in the shade. I prefer to regard the two as complementary to one another.

4. Turn right along the towpath, crossing the River Erewash. At Eastwood Lock, a footbridge carries the towpath over to the opposite bank. Continue past one bridge crossing. At a second bridge (by a cottage and caravan/boat yard) those following the shorter route will cross over for the Anchor Road parking area. Otherwise, continue along the towpath, passing beneath Langley Bridge to reach Langley Bridge Lock and the Great Northern Basin. Join the road and return to the Great Northern.

PLACES OF INTEREST

D.H. Lawrence Birthplace Museum and Durban House Heritage Centre, at Durban House, Mansfield Road, Eastwood. The Museum remains as it was in Lawrence's youth, providing a fascinating tribute to the author's life and work. The new Heritage Centre depicts the origins of Eastwood, and its links with Lawrence. Open daily from April to October 10 am to 5 pm, November to March 10 am till 4 pm. Closed over the Christmas period; charge payable. Telephone: 01773 717353.

THE BEESTON CANAL AND THE ATTENBOROUGH LAKES

Soon after entering Nottinghamshire, the Trent flows between, on one hand, the riverside meadows of Thrumpton and Barton and, on the other, the vast gravel lakes of Attenborough. With an additional stroll by the lovely Beeston Canal, this is a walk to remember.

Beeston Marina.

Within living memory this was just agricultural land, with a working ferry linking the two villages of Attenborough and Barton. Now the ferry has gone and all the farmland has been swallowed up by the quarry. But no change is, perhaps, totally bad, for where cattle used to graze, mallard and Canada geese now gather, and families relax. Much of the Trent Valley has been subjected to quarrying for gravel but it is encouraging to know that some of these areas, as here at Attenborough, can be satisfactorily converted – beautified even – as a haven for wildlife and recreation. Close by here too, at Beeston Weir, the Beeston Canal begins its short journey to its link with the surviving section of the Nottingham Canal, at Lenton. The Beeston Canal was constructed by the Trent Navigation Company in the 1790s to bypass an unnavigable stretch of the river. With the surviving section of the Nottingham Canal, this still provides a popular waterway route between Beeston and Trent Bridge, and a useful link with Nottingham City centre.

Attached to the Beeston Marina, the Tea and Coffee Shop is a busy and popular refreshment house, in pleasant surroundings overlooking the river. It offers a full menu of hot and cold meals and snacks, all at reasonable prices. Traditional Sunday lunches are a feature, as well as cream teas. Families are welcome, and so are parties.

Telephone: 0115 922 3168.

The Riverside Bar, next to the Tea and Coffee Shop, also provides food and drink.

Telephone: 0115 925 4124.

- **HOW TO GET THERE:** From Queens Road (A6005) at Beeston, follow Station Road and Meadow Road through to the end, turning right here onto Canal Side.

    Dunnline Route 2000 (Sandiacre-Stapleford-Beeston) provides an hourly bus service, Monday to Saturday only, along Canal Side.

    To Meadow Road only: Nottingham City Transport operate an hourly service from Monday to Saturday (Route 32), between Nottingham, Beeston, Stapleford and Bulwell. Bartons also provide an hourly service in the week and six Sunday journeys (Routes 18/20) between Nottingham, Beeston, Stapleford and Ilkeston.
- **PARKING:** There is adequate roadside parking space alongside the canal (Canal Side, Beeston Rylands).
- **LENGTH OF THE WALK:** 5½ miles (can be shortened to 3 miles by omitting the Beeston Canal section). The shortened version is negotiable with care, for those with wheelchairs and baby buggies. Do bear in mind, though, that most paths are over uneven, unsurfaced ground, and include two steep bridges. Maps: OS Landranger 129 Nottingham and Loughborough, OS Pathfinder 833 Nottingham South West (GR 537355).

THE WALK

1. If you are following the full route, from the western end of Canal Side, cross Beeston Lock and turn left. (For the shorter walk, begin at 3

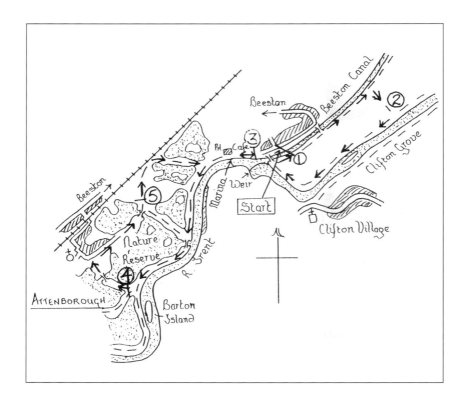

below.) Follow the elevated metalled footpath alongside the canal, and beside the recreation ground. Particularly pleasing are the beautiful overhanging weeping willows. On reaching the canal bridge, bear left a little, continuing along the towpath. Bear right again at a footbridge, rejoining the trackway and continuing ahead to a stile. Cross the stile and turn right, following the hedge and making for the river. The riverside cliff of Clifton Grove can be seen ahead, with the Teacher Training College buildings peeping over the trees to the right.

2. Turn right on reaching the River Trent. After a while, the path reverts to a gravel track, turning right with the river opposite Clifton Hall which was the home of the Clifton family from medieval times, until passing out of the family's hands in 1953, when the City Council took over most of the land here. The hall stands at the head of Clifton Grove, a broad grassy avenue, formerly of elms but now replanted with chestnuts, which follows the top of the riverside cliff. Clifton Hall is

Beeston Lock.

now an educational establishment. Continue to Beeston Weir and Lock.

3. Continue left along the riverside, passing the marina. It is very attractive here with numerous craft moored alongside. The river opens out, with wide views across towards Clifton and Barton. As the marina with its attendant boats is passed, interest is transferred to the opposite bank, with its colourful holiday chalets. And, always, there are the wildfowl – Canada geese, swans, mallard, coot – and most probably a cormorant or two – to enliven the scene.

4. Continue beside the river as far as the leftward bend by Barton Island. Turn right here, entering the nature reserve and heading towards Attenborough village church. This end of the reserve is very popular in summer, and the wildfowl take full advantage of the host of visitors. There are fine views over the water, particularly towards the village. Wildlife to look out for in the nature reserve includes foxes – and a wide variety of fish, insects and amphibia. Wildfowl identified here include sawbills, sea-ducks, garganey, cormorants and grebe. Not to mention kingfisher and heron.

After crossing a gracefully arched 'pre-fab' bridge, continue over the (private) anglers' car park to Attenborough village. Long before Trent

Gravels came on the scene, Attenborough was the home of Colonel Henry Ireton, who achieved celebrity as Oliver Cromwell's lieutenant and son-in-law. Cromwell's grandaughter was christened in the church, and we are told that Cromwell's men stabled their horses in the nave at some time during the Civil War. Turn right along the village road (The Strand). This is a cul-de-sac, but continues as a waymarked bridleway, once more within the nature reserve.

5. After crossing a second footbridge, a side-path will be seen turning off to the right. Ignore this one, keeping straight on along a well-wooded track and continuing alongside the railway for some distance. Bear away again to the right, ignoring the adjacent rail crossing and continue round, and back to the riverside. Turn left now, back to the marina and Canal Side.

PLACES OF INTEREST
Wollaton Hall, set in 500 acres of mature parkland, houses Nottingham's Natural History Museum. There are formal gardens and a fishing lake, nature trail and adventure playground. Admission to the park is free. The hall is also free in the week, but a small charge is made at weekends and bank holidays. For details, and for opening times, telephone 0115 915 3900.

WALK 4
NOTTINGHAM'S WATERWAYS
❧❀❧

The River Trent is a valued recreational facility for the people of Nottingham, and you will enjoy this interesting walk along its banks, picking out famous landmarks. Another Nottingham waterway is its canal, taking you from the river into the city itself. A fascinating way to mix town and country!

The River Trent at Nottingham.

Trent Bridge is universally famous for its Test Cricket ground. To Nottingham people, it is something more: the principal southern gateway to the city. And the place where, from time immemorial, the people have gone to relax: to fish, to cruise or to row on the river, to picnic, to listen to the band, or just to sit and watch their other, more energetic fellows. A mile or so upstream is Wilford, with its own bridge. Originally built in 1870 by a local landowner as a toll bridge (and with the tariff of tolls still displayed), the modern bridge is now reserved for pedestrians and cyclists. And, despite the long-standing presence on the northern bank of the vast and now redeveloped

Meadows residential area, Wilford village still retains its essentially rural atmosphere. The part of the Nottingham Canal followed here is the best surviving section, still used by water craft and popular with anglers.

The Toll Bridge Inn, on the Victoria Embankment, not far from the Wilford bridge and where this walk begins, is a welcoming modern Scottish and Newcastle house, overlooking the river. Bar snacks are available all through the day, and full meals from noon until 2 pm (2.30 pm at the weekend). The management are prepared, however, to open the kitchen at any time for hot meals, subject to adequate staffing levels. Walkers are especially welcome and, if a party of six or more anticipate visiting and telephone in with their expected time of arrival, the pub will open for tea, coffee or soft drinks from 8 am onwards. Meals can also be booked over the phone if arrival is likely to be outside normal kitchen hours. Telephone: 0115 986 2894.

Also recommended is the Ferry Inn, on the Main Road at Wilford and passed on the walk.

Telephone: 0115 981 1441.

- **HOW TO GET THERE:** From Trent Bridge (north side): follow Bathley Street and Bunbury Street round onto Victoria Embankment, continuing past the Memorial Gardens and Suspension Bridge, and on. The Toll Bridge Inn is on the right.

  Those relying on public transport are recommended to start the walk from Trent Bridge or from Carrington Street. Many city and county bus routes are channelled through Trent Bridge and its approaches, and routes from all areas visit the City Centre. Nottingham (Midland) Railway Station is also on the route of the main walk.

- **PARKING:** If calling there, you may use the pub car park. Otherwise, there should be roadside space available opposite. My personal preference, however, is the Wilford Bridge approach road, on the south side of the river – reached via Wilford Lane (B679) and Main Street.

- **LENGTH OF THE WALK:** 5 miles.

  If you are short of time, a straightforward, easy walk of about 3 miles, needing no detailing, could be taken along one side of the river and back along the other, between Trent Bridge and Wilford Bridge. In that case, choose your own starting point and direction of walk!

  Both routes can safely be followed by wheelchair users, subject to some manual assistance on the canal section (stepped access ramps and narrow towpath) on the longer walk.

Maps: OS Landranger 129 Nottingham and Loughborough, OS Pathfinder 833 Nottingham South West (GR 572381).

THE WALK

1. Leaving the Toll Bridge Inn, follow the footpath round its eastern edge to join Bathley Street. Continue around two sides of the recreation ground, following Wilford Grove back to the riverside and turn left.

2. Follow the Embankment, a splendid avenue of mature plane trees – or, better, the riverside path – passing the suspension bridge and the memorial gardens, and enjoying the life of the river. Wildfowl are plentiful here and you are sure to see swans, Canada geese and mallard. Depending on the season and the day of the week, there will also be anglers, rowing eights and strollers! The large building visible over the river is the County Hall with, not to be outdone, the Rushcliffe Borough Council building prominent beyond. Nottingham Forest's stadium can also be seen and, as you approach Trent Bridge, the Trent Bridge Inn and the cricket ground come into view. (Public conveniences, if required, will be found on the roadway approach to Trent Bridge – there will not be another chance before the end of the walk!)

3. Cross the road, carefully – or, for preference, return to the riverside and pass beneath the bridge, noting, as you pass, the flood levels cut into the wall. Ascend to the road, turning right and passing the Turney's Quay building. Pass the Meadow Lane junction. At the next turning – a non-vehicular traditional canal bridge – cross over and descend to join the Nottingham Canal. It is much healthier here than when we met it in the Erewash Valley (Walk 2)! Turn right and follow the towpath.

The canal here runs side by side with London Road, one of Nottingham's busiest thoroughfares. Yet it is easy to overlook – or ignore – this as you stroll idly beside the placid waterway exchanging, perhaps, a greeting with the occasional passing canal-boat. Notable landmarks to look out for as we proceed northward alongside London road include, on London Road itself, the Hicking Pentecost building of 1873, formerly a 'tenement factory', with various lace manufacturers renting accommodation. Opposite this building, on the other bank of

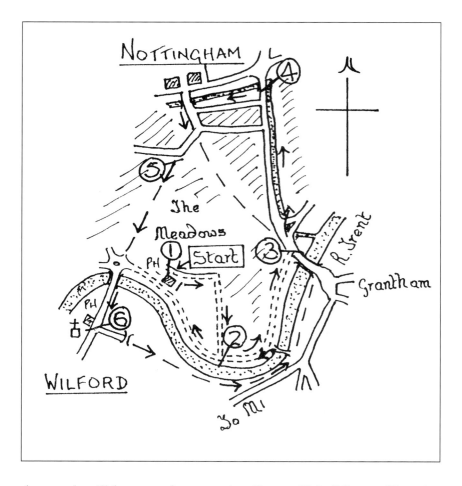

the canal, will be seen the attractive 'Eastcroft' building, a Victorian depot of the Nottingham Corporation.

4. After passing beneath the Great Northern Close bridge, the towpath crosses over to the opposite bank, and the canal swings left by the 'Island Street' site to continue, passing beneath Trent Street and on under Carrington Street. With the modern Magistrates' Court building ahead, double back left to rejoin the road and turn right. Opposite the Midland Station, turn right again, following Sheriffs Way (or the adjacent Queens Bridge Road).

5. Where the road swings right, keep straight ahead along the combined footpath/cycleway route of Queen's Walk, a pleasant, tree-lined avenue. At the end of Queen's Walk continue round the roundabout and on, crossing the Toll Bridge and continuing to the Ferry Inn.

6. Turn left opposite the inn, following Coronation Avenue. There is a footpath along the top of the floodbank on the left, which gives a good view over the Coronation Fishing Pond. Pass under the (redundant) railway bridge, and bear left past the Wilford Meadows School, following the metalled footpath. After crossing the riverside fields, with good views across the river, the path descends to an enclosed way, passing the Rivermead Flats and the Becket Upper School. Cross the suspension bridge and turn left, following the road back to the Toll Bridge Inn.

PLACES OF INTEREST

There is much in Nottingham to interest the visitor. The *Brewhouse Yard Museum* on Castle Boulevard (under the Castle Rock) occupies a group of 18th century cottages, offering a realistic picture of everyday Nottingham life over the last two centuries. Open daily 10 am to 5 pm (except Fridays between November and February, when the hours are 1 pm till 5 pm). Last admission 4.45 pm. Closed Christmas Day and Boxing Day. Telephone: 0115 915 3600. *The Tales of Robin Hood,* on Maid Marion Way (telephone 0115 948 3284) offers the opportunity to experience the sights and sounds of life as it really was in the time of Robin Hood. There are fascinating audio-visual shows, and the chance to try one's hand at archery (Shoot the Sheriff).

THE GRANTHAM CANAL IN THE VALE OF BELVOIR

After entering Nottinghamshire near Hickling, the Grantham Canal follows a serpentine course through the county en route for its discharge into the Trent near Nottingham, passing through the lovely Vale of Belvoir. Starting from Kinoulton village, this peaceful walk follows field-paths to the outskirts of Colston Bassett. Close to here, the canal path is joined on one of its most delightful stretches, as we pursue a winding route back to Kinoulton.

The Grantham Canal, Kinoulton.

The fertile and peaceful Vale of Belvoir, in the extreme south-east of the county, spans the Leicestershire county boundary. This is farming country, with lush pastures and wooded hills, and the home of Stilton cheese. The villages here are of the familiar red brick and pantiles, with few concessions to modern development. Kinoulton – where the walk commences – is a typical linear village, close to the Grantham Canal.

Though today largely a commuter village, it has a proud history. There was a castle here in the Middle Ages, and Archbishop Cranmer built a palace in the village. In Georgian times the spring on a hill to the west was famed as a spa. The Grantham Canal was opened in 1797, 33 miles long, linking Grantham town with the River Trent at Nottingham. Its principal use was the transport of corn, timber, coal, lime etc (including night-soil!) Its use declined with the advent of the railways and the canal was abandoned, for commercial purposes, in the 1930s.

The Nevile Arms, a pleasant and welcoming 'Kimberley' house, which displays the arms of the local landowners, the Earls of Gainsborough, stands at the eastern end of the main street of Kinoulton. Families are welcome here, and there is a children's play area. Well-behaved dogs are also welcome, although not in the beer garden. An impressive range of bar snacks and full meals is available, lunch-times and evenings, from Tuesday to Saturday. On Sunday and Monday, cobs only are available – and I strongly recommend the hot bacon cobs! If using the pub's facilities, you may park here for the duration of your walk – but do ask.

Telephone: 01949 81236.

Food and drink are also available, part-way around the walk (but a little off-route), at the Martin's Arms in Colston Bassett. A homely village pub, it is listed in the Les Routieres guide – and reputedly has its own resident ghost!

Telephone: 01949 81361.

- **HOW TO GET THERE:** The Widmerpool to Kinoulton road leaves the A606 (Nottingham to Melton) a little to the north-west of its junction with the A46 (Fosse Way) at Widmerpool crossroads. It crosses the Fosse Way, continuing through to Kinoulton. The walk starts from the eastern end of the main street.

  A two-hourly service by 'Roadcar' (Route 29: Nottingham-Cotgrave-Long Clawson-Hose) calls at Kinoulton, Monday to Saturday only. Barton's route 23/23a (Nottingham-Cotgrave-Kinoulton-Melton) also calls here, thrice daily from Monday to Saturday. There is no Sunday service.

- **PARKING:** If not visiting the Nevile Arms, it should be possible to find space alongside the green (by the pub, at the eastern end of Main Street).

- **LENGTH OF THE WALK:** $5\frac{1}{2}$ miles. Maps: OS Landranger 129 Nottingham and Loughborough, OS Pathfinder 834 Radcliffe on Trent, (GR 681310).

THE WALK

1. From the Nevile Arms, cross Owthorpe Lane and follow Hall Lane out of the village. The metalled road ends at Hall Farm, but continue ahead, following the waymarked bridleway route along a clear field path. As you proceed, the spire of Colston Bassett church will be seen ahead, a little to the left of the path-line. To the left of the spire is Colston Bassett Hall.

2. After passing beneath a power line, bear left from the bridleway, to reach a gateway in the far corner of the field. Through the gate, follow the hedge on your right to its end. Cross a stile and footbridge, continuing on the right of a brook, again heading towards the church spire. Towards the end of this field, pass through the gap on your left and turn right to meet – very briefly – the River Smite. Follow the hedge round left to a second gap and pass through. If you wish to visit the picturesque little village of Colston Bassett (and the Martin's Arms), you

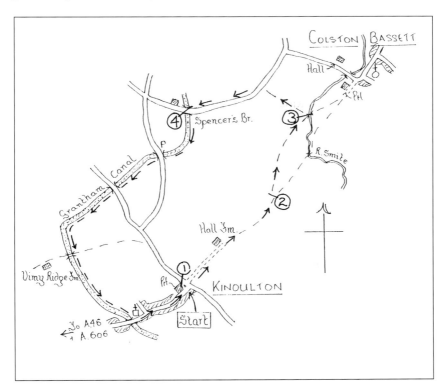

should keep straight on here, crossing the River Smite and continuing ahead. A restored medieval cross marks the centre of the village.

3. Otherwise – turn left, following the fence and succeeding hedge. At the top of the field, through a gateway, join a clear green track and continue through to the road. Turn left, following the road for a good ½ mile to meet the canal by Oddhouse Farm, at Spencer's Bridge. This survives in name only; the physical bridge, like most others along the Grantham Canal, having been removed and the canal culverted through. There are hopes that, some time, the canal will be restored to navigability (and, of course, the bridges reinstated), but that is likely to remain a long-term dream.

4. Turn left, following the canal towpath; in fair condition here, with water and wildfowl, and not too thickly overgrown, making for pleasant walking. After crossing Owthorpe Lane – where there is a public parking and picnic area – continue on to a second crossing, at Wild's Bridge. Continue, rounding the bend at Devil's Elbow, to reach Irish Jack's Bridge. Before continuing, note the avenue of poplars, on the opposite side of the canal, leading from the bridge to Vimy Ridge Farm – now abandoned. The farm was named, and the avenue planted, by Sir Jesse Hind, a prominent Nottingham solicitor, in memory of his son who died at Vimy Ridge in the 1914/18 war. Continue ahead to the road in Kinoulton village and turn left, following Main Street back to the start.

PLACES OF INTEREST

Naturescape Wild Flower Farm and Visitor Centre, at Coach Gap Lane (off Harby Road), Langar, has 40 acres of wild flower fields, with a wildlife garden, nature trail, picnic area and tea-room. Various seeds, plants etc are available for purchase and there is a small gift shop for cards and books. Open from April to September, 11 am to 5.30 pm. Admission free to wildlife garden and sales area, with a small charge for the wild flower fields, play area and pets corner from June 15 to August 15; other times free. Telephone: 01949 860592/851045.

UNSPOILT BASSINGFIELD

This pleasant and easy little country stroll links one of the most popular and best-maintained sections of the Grantham Canal with one of our smallest and sleepiest villages.

Shepherds, Stragglethorpe.

After passing through Kinoulton, the Grantham Canal winds its sinuous course past Cropwell Bishop and Cropwell Butler, before crossing the ancient Fosse Way and continuing, past the site of the former Cotgrave Colliery, to reach the hamlet of Bassingfield. For much of the way the canal is neglected and dry, but here at Bassingfield, though the bridges are gone and the locks are derelict, the water still remains; a haven for herons and other wildlife. Until very recently, the neighbouring villages of Gamston and Bassingfield were still tiny, unspoilt hamlets, with an economy based mainly on agriculture. Gamston has now disappeared under an avalanche of major roadworks and executive-type housing! Thankfully, a mile to the east and at the end of a quiet rural lane, Bassingfield retains, at least for the time being, its air of tranquil anonymity.

Shepherds Restaurant is an attractive and popular house on the busy road linking Cotgrave with the main A52. A modern conversion, the house belongs to the Whitbread's group (Miller's Kitchen) and provides an excellent and wide-ranging menu, including bar snacks and sandwiches, all at reasonable prices. Families are especially welcome here, and there is a well-equipped play area – as well as a special menu – for the kiddies. The bar is available to diners and 'non-eaters' alike, with a traditional range which includes Boddingtons, Pedigree and guest ales, as well as the usual wines, lager and ciders.
Telephone: 0115 933 3337.

- **HOW TO GET THERE:** From the A52 (Nottingham-Grantham trunk road) turn off south at the Holme House traffic lights, between Gamston Roundabout and Radcliffe on Trent, following Stragglethorpe Road. Turn right at the next junction, passing Shepherds Restaurant, and continue towards Cotgrave for a good ½ mile. The canal car park is on the right.

  Barton's 'Cotgrave Connection' operates a frequent service from Nottingham, passing Shepherds Restaurant and the canal crossing, hourly on Sundays, every 20 minutes Monday to Saturday. Barton's route 31b (Nottingham-Cotgrave-Harby) also serves this route, in the week, at peak times only.
- **PARKING:** At Cotgrave Bridge, Cotgrave Lane, Stragglethorpe, there is a small, unsurfaced, free car park in the angle of the road and the canal.
- **LENGTH OF THE WALK:** 3½ miles. Maps: OS Landranger 129 Nottingham and Loughborough, OS Pathfinder 834 Radcliffe on Trent (GR 639367).

THE WALK

1. Walk west from the car park, following the canal. The metalled footpath on the right will perhaps be preferred to the towpath (on the left), which doubles as an access track to the Lock Keeper's Cottage, with the possible intrusion of occasional vehicles. The footpath ends at the lock (sans gates!), but a footbridge crosses over to join the towpath. With the closure of the canal and the dereliction of the lock, the cottage has long since ceased to house a lock-keeper, but the name remains. And the house adds a certain charm to the scene. This section of the canal, between Cotgrave Bridge and Tollerton Lane, is one of the better stretches, with a satisfactory level of water. And, judging from the number of anglers, plenty of fish. The bird-life, too, is plentiful.

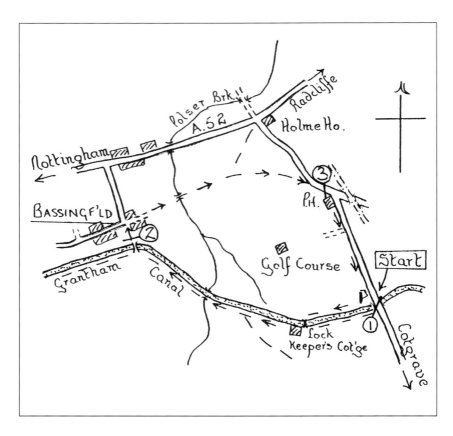

Mainly the ubiquitous mallard and coot, but swans and heron are by no means strangers here. This part of the canal is also popular with the general public, no doubt due to its close proximity to the residential areas of Cotgrave, Radcliffe and Gamston.

Continue along the tow-path, the hamlet of Bassingfield coming in view ahead and to the right. To the left of the canal, also ahead, is Nottingham Airport – a small, private field not to be confused with East Midlands Airport at Castle Donington. Nottingham Airport, formerly Tollerton Aerodrome, caters mainly for light aircraft, of which many will be seen circling around of a fine summer weekend.

2. A farm track from Bassingfield crosses the canal from right to left. Cross over and follow the track up to the village, turning right along Nathan's Lane. Past the few houses, the lane reverts to a field track and

The Grantham Canal.

continues ahead. Cross the Polser Brook and continue beside a banked area, then bear right with the track. Where the track bends left again, leave via a footpath on the right, crossing the field, corner to corner, on a well-trodden footpath. Cross a stile to join the road and turn right, following the grass verge round to Shepherds Restaurant.

3. Continue along the road – there is a good footway now – for about ½ to ¾ mile, back to the canal car park.

PLACES OF INTEREST
Holme Pierrepont National Water Sports Centre and Country Park offers 270 acres of parklands suitable for country walks and picnics. There is a nature reserve and a fishing lagoon, and a wide variety of plants and animals. The Water Sports Centre features an Olympic standard watersports course for national and international events, as well as a canoe slalom course. Open daily during daylight hours; admission free, except for certain special events. Telephone: 0115 982 1212.

VIEWS FROM THE CLIFF-SIDE AT RADCLIFFE ON TRENT

A delightful walk which offers a high-level stroll along a popular cliff-walk with tantalising glimpses, through the trees, of glorious views across the Trent river valley. The circular route is completed by more riverside walking and a visit to the charming village of Shelford; and, probably, a glimpse or two of the ubiquitous squirrels!

Riverside fields, Shelford.

Radcliffe on Trent is one of Nottinghamshire's larger villages, having developed as a result of its convenience to the city of Nottingham and its situation adjacent to the busy A52 trunk road. It is a place for which this writer has a particular affection, having worked there, in the past, for a number of years; a warm and friendly community, with no false barriers of class. Despite its size, Radcliffe still retains the essential rural character of a traditional English village, with many of the amenities, and few of the disadvantages, of suburbia. And the surrounding villages

– Holme Pierrepont, Shelford, the Cropwells to name just a few – are incomparable havens of charm and peace. Radcliffe church is a relatively modern (19th century) building, the most eye-catching feature of which is its unusual 'saddle-back' tower. The church replaces an earlier building, and contains an inscription concerning Stephen de Radcliffe, of 1245. It is said that an oaken figure of Stephen used to lie in a recess of the old church, until local excitement at a victory over the French led to his being removed, dressed as Napoleon, and ceremoniously cremated!

Radcliffe is well-endowed with refreshment facilities, possessing no fewer than four pubs, all worthy of recommendation. The most convenient, from the point of view of the walk, is the Manvers Arms, opposite the parish church on Main Road. This attractive, traditional village pub dates back to the 18th century. A Greenalls house, the range of real ales changes every week. Meals and bar snacks are provided every lunchtime, including a traditional Sunday lunch, and evenings from Monday to Saturday.

Telephone: 0115 933 2404.

- **HOW TO GET THERE:** Radcliffe on Trent is just off the A52 (Nottingham to Grantham) road, about 5 miles east of Trent Bridge.

  A regular daily 'Pathfinder' bus service between Nottingham and Newark calls at Radcliffe. The village is also served by Barton's hourly service between Nottingham and Bingham (Monday to Saturday only). The Nottingham to Grantham rail service also calls here.
- **PARKING:** There is a free public car park in the centre of the village, accessed via Richmond Terrace, opposite the Shelford Road junction. The route of the walk is described from here, but some time and distance can be saved by parking on the roadside (by the play area) on Wharf Lane.
- **LENGTH OF THE WALK:** 6 miles. Maps: OS Landranger 129 Nottingham and Loughborough, OS Pathfinder 813 Carlton and Elston and 834 Radcliffe on Trent (GR 646392).

THE WALK

1. From the car park, join Main Road and turn left, passing the Manvers Arms on your right. Immediately beyond here, and opposite the church, turn right to follow Wharf Lane as far as the railway bridge.

2. Under the bridge, join the waymarked footpath on the right,

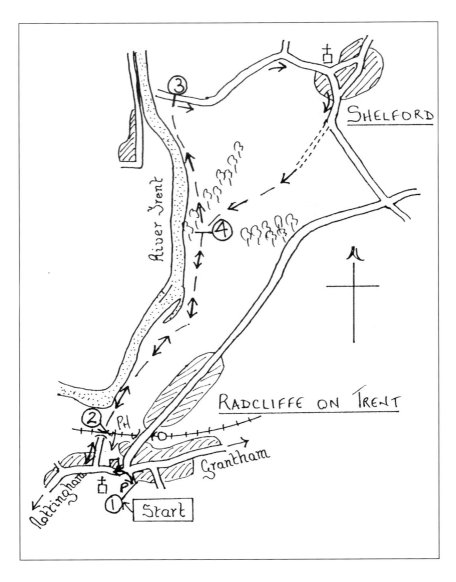

climbing up by the stepped way onto the cliff top, and a metalled avenue. The cliff – very steep, but fenced for safety – is well-wooded, but you will be able to enjoy frequent tantalising glimpses of the splendid views over the River Trent flood plain, with a broad sweep of the river flowing between low lying fields from the direction of

Young walkers at Shelford.

Nottingham, passing beneath the Nottingham-Grantham railway line and on past the Wharf Lane Caravan site, to pass below the cliff and by Stoke (Bardolph) Lock. There are also vast numbers of grey squirrels along this section of the walk. Take care not to fall over them!

After passing the park entrance, an inviting stepped path on the left suggests an alternative route. But be warned – this appears to be no more than an access route to the riverside mainly for anglers. There is no through route. Beyond the last elements of Radcliffe, the metalled path gives place to a gravel track. Then it becomes a field path, descending towards the riverside. Cross a stile and follow the flood bank path through to Stoke Ferry Lane.

3. Turn right here and continue to Shelford village. Shelford is a quiet backwater, partly because it occupies Crown land which, so far, appears to have protected it from large-scale development. An interesting reflection of this is that the current population is around 250 – much the same as it was at the time of the Domesday survey. But modern pressures inevitably lead one to wonder how long this happy position can hold? Shelford life has not always been peaceful though. At the time of the Civil War, a fierce battle in the area of the church wiped out a garrison of 200 Royalists, and led to the destruction of the

Manor House. The church – well worth a visit – has a massive perpendicular tower, which is a conspicuous landmark in the Trent valley.

Bear right along West Street, and right again at the road junction by the war memorial. Pass Bosworth Farm and, on the next bend, turn off right, following the waymarked 'footpath' route along a farm track. Where the track bends right, keep straight forward, now following a field path. You may find this somewhat overgrown after a while, but should have no difficulty following the correct line, provided you keep to the right, with the hedge and the succeeding fence.

4. This will bring you back to a stile, on your right (don't cross it!). Here your outward route is rejoined, to enjoy from a different direction those wonderful views for the rest of the journey back to Radcliffe.

PLACES OF INTEREST
Holme Pierrepont Hall is an early Tudor brick-built manor house, housing a fine collection of period furniture and artworks, as well as having a listed courtyard garden. Home-made teas. For details of opening hours and charges, telephone 0115 933 2371.

THE RIVER TRENT AT GUNTHORPE

A peaceful stroll along one of the most popular and unspoilt stretches of riverside in Nottinghamshire, with an easy crossing of open fields completing the circle and two attractive villages to visit.

Gunthorpe marina

The village of Gunthorpe traditionally has been one of Nottinghamshire's most popular picnic spots, and its popularity persists today, despite the many modern counter-attractions on offer. There is an attractively landscaped lock here, complementing the broad Gunthorpe Weir, a marina, and a beautiful stretch of riverside for the walker or idler. The busy character of Gunthorpe is nicely counterbalanced by the quiet peace of its neighbour, the unspoilt village of Caythorpe, an attractive little settlement, with a small chapel and a pub as well as the usual cottages and farms. Two small waterways – the Dover Beck and the Car Dyke – unite here. It is one of the many places in England associated with the celebrated highwayman, Dick Turpin.

There is no lack of refreshment houses along the way today. A particularly attractive watering hole, midway through the walk, is the Black Horse, Caythorpe's traditional and welcoming village pub. A feature of the house is Dick's Cupboard – where Turpin is said to have hidden. It is also claimed that a 'cloaked figure' has been seen in the 'snug' – but that could have been the writer, caped up against the elements on the day we called! The Black Horse claims to be a true free house, the home of Caythorpe Brewery and 'Dover Beck Bitter' – named after the local stream. Food is served every lunchtime from Tuesday to Saturday, and every evening except Sunday. Booking is essential in the evening when specialities are the order of the day: curry on Monday; fresh fish on Wednesday, Thursday and Friday; and 'various' on Saturday.

Telephone: 0115 966 3520.

In Gunthorpe itself are the Anchor Inn on Main Street (telephone: 0115 966 3292), Tom Brown's Bar, Trentside (telephone: 0115 966 3642); and the Unicorn Hotel, Gunthorpe Bridge (telephone: 0115 966 3612). All provide food for the visitor, as also does the Toll House Restaurant, further along the road, by the marina (telephone: 0115 966 3409).

- **HOW TO GET THERE:** The village of Gunthorpe is situated on the eastern side of the A6097 (Bingham to Oxton) road. There are two access roads. If coming from the south, turn off immediately after crossing Gunthorpe Bridge; if from the north, the turning is a mile to the south of the Lowdham (A612) roundabout.

  Barton's provide an hourly bus service, Monday to Saturday, between Nottingham, Radcliffe, Gunthorpe and East Bridgford, with a single evening run. There is no Sunday service.
- **PARKING:** The car park opposite the Unicorn Hotel is private – for customers only. There is a public car park further along the riverside road, by the marina and Gunthorpe Lock.
- **LENGTH OF THE WALK:** 3½ miles. Maps: OS Landranger 129 Nottingham and Loughborough, OS Pathfinder 813 Carlton and Elston (GR 686437).

THE WALK

1. Turn left out of the car park, following the riverside meadow path. This is a pleasant path, with easy access between the fields via the traditional double swing-gates. You may be lucky enough to see the

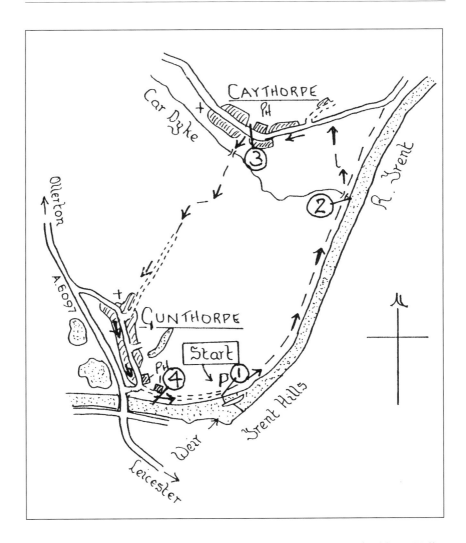

lock being negotiated, and there are good views over to the Trent Hills, on the East Bridgford side of the river.

2. After passing beneath power lines, cross the Car Dyke (twin gates), and bear left over the flood bank to reach a bridle gate in the angle of the hedge. The River Trent flows through a broad plain, which has always been subject to flooding. Particularly severe flooding in 1946 and 1947 led to the improvement of flood prevention measures throughout the county, and today there is a floodbank along one or both banks of the Trent for most, if not all, of its length. A side-effect of the embankment (also evident alongside the Soar) is the availability of an elevated walkway. Through the bridle gate, continue to the field, turning right and following the hedge to the road. Turn left and follow the road into Caythorpe village.

3. Almost directly opposite the Black Horse, turn left onto the waymarked path beside the Old Mill, passing between buildings and entering the fields. Follow the left of the hedge, transferring to the right after re-crossing Car Dyke.

After two more fields, turn right with the track. Then turn left again at the end of the field, beside a young (1998) wood. Meet a metalled lane, and follow through to Gunthorpe village, turning left here to reach the riverside.

4. Turn left now. The road runs through to the car park, but for a more pleasant route join the riverside path, via the Unicorn car park, passing the marina to rejoin the road further on.

PLACES OF INTEREST
Ferry Farm Country Park and Restaurant, at Boat Lane, Hoveringham (follow the road through Caythorpe and on beside the river) is open from late March to the end of September (not Monday, except Bank Holidays), from 10 am until 5.30 pm. There are farm animals, rare breeds, a pets' corner, activity playgroup and assault course, and a wildlife pond, as well as an extensive gift shop and tea room. The restaurant is open in the evenings for larger parties, and a menu is available on request. Admission charge. Telephone: 0115 966 5037/4512.

WALK 9

THE EDINGLEY BECK

The little River Greet enters the Trent between Gunthorpe and Newark having, in the course of its journey, gathered up the Edingley Beck. The waterways in this delightful area of central Nottinghamshire are modest and secretive, but you will still find one or two charming ponds along the way! Apart from that, the hills are gentle, the paths are well marked, and the walk is perfection.

Kirklington fish-pond.

The villages of Kirklington and Edingley nestle in the very heart of central Nottinghamshire, an area of rolling hills, pleasant woods, and vast open fields. This is essentially agricultural country, although most people nowadays commute for work to places as diverse as Southwell, Mansfield, Nottingham – and London. But that is the pattern everywhere, on the rim of the millennium. Kirklington, outwardly a purely traditional Nottinghamshire village, nevertheless boasted some interesting customs in past years. Such as the annual letting of the village roads, for grazing, between May and September. And the slaughter and distribution of a fat, estate-fed beast among the villagers, according to family size, every Christmas. A particularly delightful tale tells of a 19th century rector, who used to remove the pulpit from its base on weekdays, to serve as a hide for duck-shooting on a local swamp area.

Kirklington, on the A617, is the larger of the two villages, but boasts no refreshment facilities. For these you must go to Edingley, where the Old Reindeer on Main Street – a delightful 18th century local with comfortable accommodation and a separate restaurant – provides a truly friendly and obliging welcome, cheerful service and excellent value. Freshly prepared food is available every lunchtime from Tuesday to Sunday (cold snacks on Monday); and evenings from Tuesday to Saturday. A varied menu offers a full four-course meal or a two-course luncheon, as well as a vast array of main courses – flesh, fish or fowl, and a good range of chef's specials from the blackboard. There is a satisfying selection, too, of filled baps and bar snacks, and ploughman's lunches. The pub has a lovely garden for the children, and a pond, complete with ducks. There is a non-smoking area, an outside drinking area, and well-behaved dogs are welcome in the tap-room.

Telephone: 01623 882253.

- **HOW TO GET THERE:** Edingley is on the unclassified Rainworth to Southwell road, about 2 miles east of Farnsfield. From the A614 (Nottingham/Doncaster) road, turn east at the White Post roundabout.
  The village is served by Stagecoach East Midlands buses, with a frequent daily service (hourly, Monday to Saturday; two-hourly on Sundays) between Newark, Southwell and Mansfield.
- **PARKING:** At the Old Reindeer, in Edingley, if using the pub facilities. If not, you may park at the Southwell Trail car park and picnic area, Kirklington (GR 676566) following the walk route from there.
- **LENGTH OF THE WALK:** 5 miles. Maps: OS Landranger 120 Mansfield and Worksop, OS Explorer 28 Sherwood Forest (GR 664560).

THE WALK

1. Follow the road south-east from the Old Reindeer. Ignore the first guidepost on the left, by the Methodist chapel and opposite the parish church, continuing to a second guidepost, giving direct access to the Edingley Beck-side path. In high summer you may find the beck rather heavily overgrown with very little evidence of water, but the colourful water plants are a delight in themselves. The path is clear, with excellent stiles.

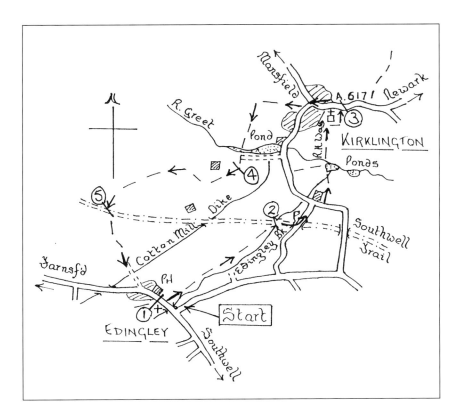

2. At the Southwell Trail (which follows the route of the old Mansfield to Rolleston railway line), turn right through the car park and join the road; then left, towards Kirklington. Turn right at the next road junction, the Southwell turning, passing Osmanthorpe Manor on your left, then left onto the waymarked footpath (Robin Hood Way). Follow the fieldside path to a footbridge; cross and continue beside a fish-pond to a second footbridge, over the River Greet. Over the bridge, bear left with the path over the field, passing through a gap and continuing, with the hedge now on your right, towards Kirklington church. Turn right and left past a house and follow the residential road to Kirklington's main street (the A617), against the church. Turn left.

3. Turn left again onto Southwell Road, leaving it on the right via a green track (waymarked footpath) on the bend. This leads to an ascending path over open fields. Immediately after passing a clump of trees on your left, turn left and continue, initially with a hedge on your left. When this ends, keep straight forward over a vast open 'prairie', with magnificent wide views in every direction. At the far side of the field, bear left with the line of the trees, looking out for a waymarked gap. This leads, via a couple of steps or so, into a delightful woodland path, crossing an ancient mill-pond, complete with a family of swans when we came, to reach a farm road.

4. Cross the road and continue on the waymarked line, following the hedge on your right and turning sharp right with the hedge. Pass to the left of Moor Farm and continue to the end of the field. Bear right, now with the hedge on your left, with an overhead power line keeping close company. As the power line leads away right and the hedge ends, bear left diagonally, as indicated by a yellow arrow sign, to reach a short length of track. From here, the path continues, still diagonally, over a large field, making for a distant tree corresponding to an angle in the hedge. At the corner of the hedge, bear left a little, passing between the tree and the near hedge to reach and cross the Southwell Trail, as directed by a pair of guide posts.

5. Immediately after crossing the trail turn left, then right, down the field with the hedge on your right. Some way down the field, bear left, following a clear, well waymarked and trodden path through the fields, to join a farm track. Cross Cotton Mill Dyke and continue through to Edingley Main Street, turning left for the Old Reindeer.

PLACES OF INTEREST

West of Edingley, near the White Post roundabout, the *Wonderland Pleasure Park* offers a glorious variety of family entertainment in 30 acres of parkland. There is a nine hole golf course (and crazy golf), a giant sandpit, a huge bouncy castle, and much besides. Telephone: 01623 882773. The *White Post Modern Farm Centre,* in the same area, is a working farm with displays and exhibitions, where visitors can meet over 4,000 animals of all kinds – including llamas. There are picnic sites and indoor areas, including a reptile house, as well as a gift shop and tea rooms. Telephone: 01623 882977.

THE SOUTHWELL TRAIL AND THE RIVER GREET

A short and sweet little walk from the charming old town of Southwell, combining the sylvan delights of a footpath created along a former railway track with the riparian pleasures of one of Nottinghamshire's least known rivers.

The River Greet at Maythorne.

Southwell is home to the impressive 12th century Minster, the seat of the Bishops of the Anglican diocese of Southwell. With many ancient and beautiful buildings, there is much of interest to be seen by the visitor, including the splendid half-timbered Saracen's Head Hotel, where Charles I stayed in 1646, before surrendering to his enemies. Southwell is also the 'birthplace' of the Bramley Apple – part of the original tree being still in existence. There are a host of pleasant footpaths in and around the surrounding fields and villages, particularly alongside the River Greet. How to pronounce the town's name is a long-standing bone of contention. The locals say it as it is spelt: South Well; but visitors, 'off-comers', and race-goers call it Suthall. You pays your money and you takes your choice! The former Mansfield to Rolleston railway line has been out of use for many years, but its trackbed provides the route for the Southwell Trail, one of Nottinghamshire's oldest and most successful recreational railway routes.

The most convenient 'water-hole' for this walk, lying adjacent to the Southwell Trail Car Park, is the Newcastle Arms on Station Road. Regrettably, this friendly and attractive Greenalls house does not provide food – although there is no objection to genuine patrons picnicking at the tables on the lawns, overlooking the trail. There is a children's play area. Opening hours in the week are from 12 noon until 2 pm and 5.30 pm to 11 pm. Sunday hours are from noon until 3 pm and 7 pm to 10.30 pm.

Telephone: 01636 813094.

There is no shortage of alternative pubs, which do provide food, in Southwell town centre (½ mile away). But a particularly attractive and excellent venue is the Minster Refectory which, as the name indicates, is within the Minster grounds. A friendly welcome awaits the visitor in clean, modern surroundings, most people's appetites being catered for with a range of mouth-watering delicacies, including vegetarian dishes. Opening hours are from 9.30 am until 5.30 pm in the week, and noon until 5.30 pm on Sunday (winter closing at 5 pm). Children and the disabled are catered for, and party bookings are accepted.

Telephone: 01636 815691.

- **HOW TO GET THERE:** Southwell lies on the main A612 road and, if coming from the Nottingham direction, this is the most direct route. Those coming from Newark or Mansfield will follow the A617, joining the A612 between Averham and Hockerton.

  There are regular daily bus services, including Sunday, between Nottingham, Southwell and Newark (Pathfinder), and between Newark, Southwell and Mansfield (Stagecoach East Midlands). These connect with the town centre, ½ mile from the start of the walk.
- **PARKING:** In the Southwell Trail Car Park, Station Road, Southwell.
- **LENGTH OF THE WALK:** 2½ miles. Maps: OS Landranger 120 Mansfield and Worksop, OS Pathfinder 796 Newark on Trent West (GR 706544).

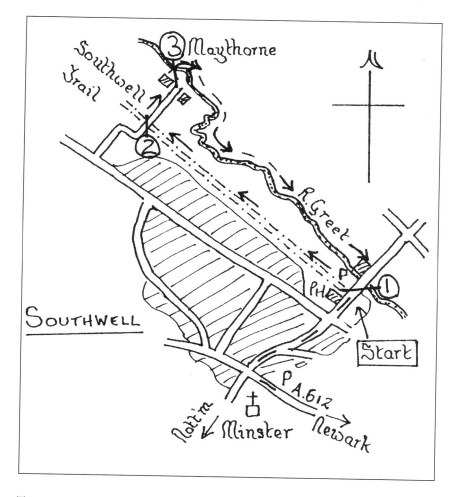

THE WALK

1. Leave the car park, following the straight and narrow pathway of the Trail. The former railway fell to the Beeching Axe, back in the 1960s, and was subsequently dedicated as a public footpath. Over the years the trackway has been taken over by Nature, developing into a botanist's delight, with just a narrow footway down the centre for public enjoyment.

2. On reaching a road (Maythorne Lane), leave the Southwell Trail. Turn right, to Maythorne Mill, a former textile mill now converted to

Maythorne

industrial and residential units. It is quite an attractive little estate today, with a caravan site and a large pond. The River Greet flows close by, providing a home for a family of ducks. Follow the road between the buildings, bearing left at the end to cross the river.

3. Turn right and follow the hedge, crossing a footbridge at the top of the field and continuing round to the right, by the riverside field path. The River Greet follows a tortuous route, the path meandering faithfully alongside. The nettles, in season, can be a little troublesome! Join the road at Greet Lily Mill (a former corn mill, this one) and turn right, back to the car park.

PLACES OF INTEREST
Magnificent *Southwell Minster,* the cathedral church of the diocese of Southwell, is always open to visitors. But please remember, especially if a service is in progress when you come, that this is an active place of worship – due reverence is expected. The *Bramley Apple Exhibition,* at the Merryweather Garden Centre in Southwell (telephone: 01636 813204) traces the history and development of the Bramley. Open daily from 9 am until 5 pm, admission free.

TOWN AND COUNTRY AT NEWARK
❧❧❧

*West of Newark, the River Trent branches, one arm flowing north via
Kelham to rejoin the other – the Newark Branch – near Winthorpe.
The Newark Branch itself flows by the town, passing beneath the
great wall of the castle, the grounds of which can be visited on this
fascinating mix of rural and urban walking.*

Newark Town Lock.

The ancient market town of Newark is one of the county's most
beautiful, with a magnificent heritage of ancient and attractive
buildings. One of the most striking is the ancient castle, on the
riverside, particularly noteworthy as the place of King John's death in
1216. The castle itself is not open to the public at present, although the
grounds are, and these alone are well worth a visit. The Gilstrap
Centre, within the castle grounds, will also repay a little of your time,
with its multi-media exhibition telling the Newark Castle Story. A
diversion into the town centre via Kirkgate can be very rewarding. The
parish church of St Mary Magdalene is said to be the finest in

Nottinghamshire, with a spire which dominates the town. The oldest part of the building is the 12th century crypt, which houses the treasury, where some of the church's plate is on display. The 14th/15th century stained glass in the east window of the south chapel is also worth viewing. The market place is particularly interesting, the many fine buildings including three historic inns; the White Hart, the Saracen's Head, and the Clinton Arms, which have played host to such notables as Sir Walter Scott, Lord Byron, and Gladstone.

The Castle Barge is unique; a popular, flower-bedecked, floating public house moored near Newark Castle, where you have the choice of dining 'tween decks' or 'onshore'. Built in 1913 as a grain barge, she was converted into a pub in 1980, with instant success. This is one of Mansfield Brewery's 'houses', with opening hours from 11 am to 11 pm in the week, and from noon until 10.30 pm on Sunday. Tea and coffee are served throughout the day, with food available daily from noon until 2 pm and evenings from 5 pm till 7 pm. There is a full range of appetizing meals and bar snacks on offer, all freshly prepared to order. And there is a special kiddies menu too.

Telephone: 01636 706333.

- **HOW TO GET THERE:** The A46 (Leicester-Newark-Lincoln) road follows the Newark Northern Bypass. Where the A616 (Ollerton) and A617 (Mansfield) roads join the bypass, turn south-east, following this road into Newark. A turning on the right (Tolney Lane), immediately before the river bridge, gives access to the long-stay car park, and the riverside park.

  Newark is well served with bus services from all surrounding towns – Nottingham, Mansfield, Southwell, Lincoln, etc. The Nottingham to Lincoln rail service also calls here, stopping at Newark Castle station, close to the start of the walk.
- **PARKING:** Tolney Lane car park – as above.
- **LENGTH OF THE WALK:** 2½ miles. Maps: OS Landranger 121 Lincoln, OS Pathfinder 796 Newark on Trent West and 797 Newark on Trent East (GR 795541).

THE WALK

1. Leaving the car park, cross the main road, following the riverside track, with modern blocks of flats on your left. Continue past former warehouses, now either restored or converted, and on along the ensuing field-path, passing beneath a redundant railway bridge.

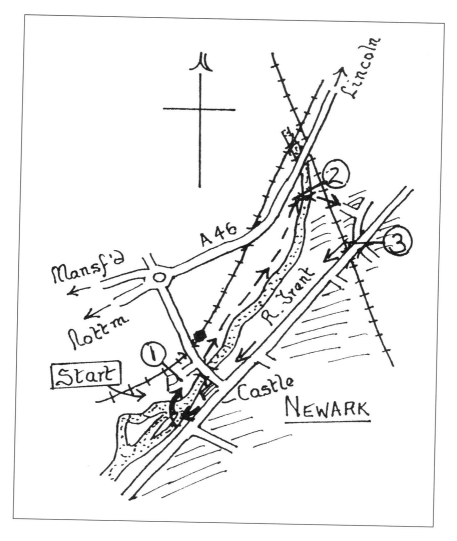

2. Cross the river via a graceful single-arch footbridge, continuing straight ahead along the waymarked bridleway route, past derelict industrial buildings. Cross the railway line *with great care* – and only if the green light is showing. This is a very fast line, with High Speed Trains operating. Continue ahead along Hatchets Lane (residential), turning right at the end, and continuing to an underpass.

Newark Castle.

3. Ascend to the road (Lincoln Road Bridge) and turn right, crossing the railway and continuing, via Northgate, back to the Castle Gate/Bar Gate junction. Northgate, with Castlegate, has many 17th and 18th century buildings, reflecting in particular Newark's brewing heritage. This stretch of road follows the line of the Roman Fosse Way and, by the castle, crosses the former Great North Road. Cross Market Hill and enter the castle grounds. Newark Castle was built around 1130 and it was here, in 1216, that King John died. Keep to the right by the castle keep, descending to the riverside. Continue ahead and round by Newark Town Lock, crossing over to the opposite bank and returning to the car park.

PLACES OF INTEREST

The *Millgate Museum of Social and Folk Life,* at 48 Millgate, Newark (telephone: 01636 679403) is a fascinating evocation of life – streets, shops and houses – in the Victorian and Edwardian periods. Open Monday to Friday, 10 am till 5 pm; Saturday and Sunday 1 pm till 5 pm – latest admission 4.30 pm. Admission free. *Newark Air Museum,* at the Airfield, Winthorpe is the largest volunteer-managed aviation museum in Great Britain. Telephone 01636 707170 for details of opening hours and admission charges.

WALK 12

CROSSING THE FLEET

This walk is a peaceful and relaxing blend of quiet lanes, pleasant field-paths and traditional riverside meadows with placidly grazing cattle.

The Horse Pool, near Collingham.

After Newark, the Trent turns north and, for much of its journey, forms the county boundary with Lincolnshire. For this reason, the old-world village of Collingham, lying as it does to the east of the river, probably has more in common with Lincoln than with Nottingham. This is a mainly agricultural area although, as in so many other areas up and down the Trent valley, the quarrying of gravel has left – and continues to leave – its mark. Collingham is really two villages, with two parish churches – North Collingham and South Collingham, which united in 1974 – but it would be difficult to determine where South terminates and North commences! Collingham is likewise threaded by two principal streets. The main road – the A1133 – is clearly the busiest, where all the shops, the pubs, and the village businesses are. Just to the west, and blessedly ignored by the 'passing-through' motorist, Low Street is completely different: traditional, residential, unspoilt and quiet. Just south of the Grey Horse, on High Street, is the stump of a Saxon cross. There are a number of good Georgian buildings in High Street and Low Street. The Old Hall in Low Street is believed to be the birthplace of John Blow, the composer, and teacher of Henry Purcell. The Fleet (crossed during the walk) was the old course – before 1600 – of the River Trent.

At the north end of Collingham, the Grey Horse is an attractive Scottish and Newcastle house, with comfortable, homely facilities indoors, and beautiful floral hanging baskets outside. There is a children's play area and an outside drinking area, and there is no objection to visiting walkers leaving their vehicles here for the duration of the walk. Food is available daily (including Sunday) from 12 noon until 2 pm, with a range of bar food and filled rolls. There is a separate children's menu, as well as vegetarian dishes.

Telephone: 01636 892330.

- **HOW TO GET THERE:** Via the A46 (Leicester-Newark-Lincoln) road, turning off onto the A1133 (Gainsborough road) at Winthorpe, north of Newark. The Grey Horse is on the A1133 at the north end of Collingham.

  Wrights of Newark operate six bus runs daily (Monday to Saturday) between Newark, Collingham and Harby. This is supplemented by Roadcar (between Newark and Collingham only) with an hourly service in the evening and two-hourly on Sunday. There is also an hourly 'shuttle' service in the week between Newark and Collingham.
- **PARKING:** Apart from the pub car park, there is ample on-street parking space along the adjacent section of Low Street.
- **LENGTH OF THE WALK:** 4½ miles. Maps: OS Landranger 121 Lincoln and surrounding area, OS Pathfinder 781 Lincoln South (GR 832624).

THE WALK

1. From the Grey Horse, follow Low Street as far as All Saints church, crossing the road to examine the inscriptions in the wall beside the southern entrance gate to the church. These mark the heights to which, over the years, the River Trent has risen. The most significant of these dates back to 1795, but quite serious flooding occurred also in 1875 and 1947. Recross the road, and take the side turning opposite the church, crossing the Fleet. Keep to the metalled lane round a

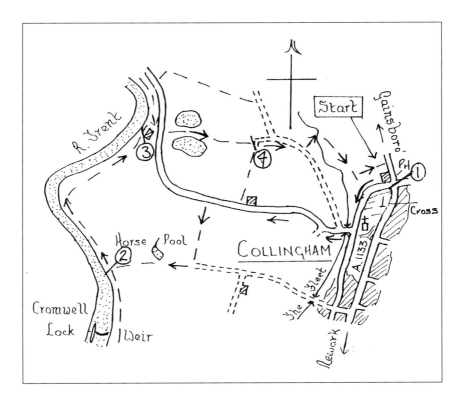

double bend, passing beneath a power line and Ferry Lane Farm. At a 'Bridleway' guidepost, turn left onto a field track, continuing to the junction with Westfield Lane. Turn right here, negotiating a double bend by Horse Pool and continuing to the river.

2. Turn right onto the flood bank, following the riverside path downstream. This is a pleasant stretch of the now-tidal Trent, with gentle cattle grazing the fields, a handful of anglers, and only the quiet hum, in the background, of traffic on the A1, out of sight over the river.

3. After passing Wharf Cottage and Bungalow (on your right), double back right beside a paddock to reach a stile, leading into Carlton Ferry Lane. Cross the lane and continue ahead on the waymarked footpath, passing between a pair of lakes (former gravel workings). At the end of the lakes, bear right with the path, then left over a footbridge. Continue straight ahead now, with the hedge on your left.

59

4. Reaching a green lane, turn left, then right with the lane, keeping straight on along gravelled Northcroft Lane to reach a waymarked footpath (kissing gate) on your left. Cross the field and a footbridge. Then bear right, continuing down the field to reach a three-way guidepost, just short of a farm gate. Turn left and follow the field path. This leads into a narrow beckside path (take care!) and thence to the A1133 just outside North Collingham. Turn right now, back to the Grey Horse.

PLACES OF INTEREST

A few miles north of Collingham, at North Clifton, the *Pureland Japanese Garden and Relaxation Centre* was created out of a derelict field by the efforts of a single man, with no previous experience of building or gardening work. The result is truly inspiring and stunningly beautiful. The garden is open from April to October, Tuesday to Saturday, between 1 pm and 5.30 pm. The Meditation Centre is open all year, by arrangement. Light refreshments are available. Telephone: 01777 228567.

VICAR WATER AND SPA PONDS
❦

Discover the beauty that exists within a short distance of one of Nottinghamshire's last surviving working collieries on this walk by the River Maun and the delightfully named Vicar Water.

Vicar Water

The north-west of the county has a cluster of rivers – the Maun, Meden, Poulter, Ryton – all of which come together to form the Idle. Which, in turn, will feed the Trent. The Maun is perhaps the best known of these since it passes through, and explains the name of, one of our main towns: Mansfield. Just down the road from Mansfield, the story of Clipstone is irrevocably bound in with that of the ancient Royal Forest of Sherwood. King John had a 'palace' here; a hunting lodge which is acknowledged to have existed even before his own day. Today there are two Clipstones – the 'Old' and the 'New'. Old Clipstone, from which we begin the walk, is still a tiny, relatively unspoilt village on the busy 'B' road between Mansfield and Ollerton. A mile or two nearer to Mansfield, the much larger town of New Clipstone owes its existence

61

to the local colliery, happily still operating. Despite the presence of the pit, there is still beauty here. The River Maun, with its accompanying Flood Dike, flows close by and, together with the delightful Vicar Pond, provides ideal conditions for the angler. And the forest, with a wealth of tracks for walking and cycling, is all around.

The Dog and Duck, at Old Clipstone, is a welcoming Scottish and Newcastle house with a well-earned reputation for good food and drink. Home-cooked food is available from Monday to Saturday between 12 noon and 2.30 pm, and from 6 pm until 9 pm, with a traditional roast on Sunday. A special recommendation is the home-made steak and kidney pie, or large cod in batter. Or you may choose from the various daily specials. 'Lite Bites' include a selection of fresh filled rolls, jacket potatoes, rump steak bap, or a chip cob. There is a special chidren's menu too. Speciality ales include Cask Home Bitter and Theakston's XB. There is a family room as well as a children's play area, and an outside drinking area.

Telephone: 01623 822138

- **HOW TO GET THERE:** Old Clipstone is on the B6030 road from Mansfield, which connects with the A614 about a mile south of Ollerton. Alternatively, if coming from the Nottingham direction, turn left at the 'Rose Cottage' (B6034), turning left again at the traffic lights.

  Stagecoach East Midlands operate a good daily bus service, Sundays included, between Mansfield and Ollerton, and calling at Clipstone.
- **PARKING:** The Dog and Duck's car park is available to patrons. For those not visiting the pub, there is a public parking area immediately to the rear of the pub car park, and adjacent to the start of the 'Vicar's Water' path.
- **LENGTH OF THE WALK:** 7 miles. Maps: OS Landranger 120 Mansfield and Worksop, OS Explorer 28 Sherwood Forest (GR 606649).

THE WALK

1. Follow the gravelled bridleway immediately to the rear of the Dog and Duck. The map shows this as running parallel to a stream – Vicar Water, but this is not visible at this point, and is probably dry or overgrown. Do not despair – it will appear in due course! Looking over the fields here, beyond Vicar Water, the ruins of King John's Palace will be seen on the top of a rise. Regrettably, there appears to be no access to the ruins, other than by trespass over private arable fields. The colliery workings soon come into view ahead and to the right. Ignore a

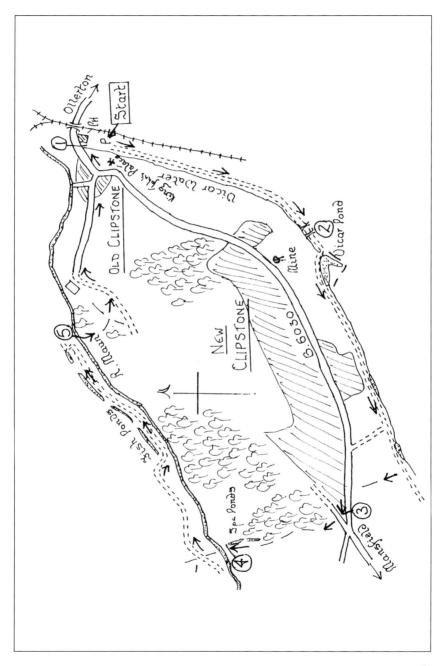

Maun Fisheries, Clipstone.

waymarked turning on the right, and pass a refrigeration engineer's buildings on your left. Continue ahead, still on the gravelled track.

2. After passing beneath a couple of railway bridges, you arrive at Vicar Pond. This is a beautiful site, with anglers, picnickers, and wildfowl; all in a woodland setting, and overlooked – but not overshadowed – by the colliery headstocks! The main track passes round to the right of the lake. For better views, however – and pleasanter walking – keep to the left; the footpath way. After crossing an arm of the water, continue to a footbridge, cross over to rejoin the road, and turn left. Continue ahead through a tunnel and past a housing estate, keeping straight on as the road reverts to a track. On past Bridleways Guest House and Newlands Farm, with Newlands Fishing Lakes on the left. At a bridle gate turn right, following a green lane up the hill to meet the road (B6030).

3. Cross the road, go through the hedge and turn left, following the road to the next junction, Clipstone Drive. Turn right here, leaving soon via a waymarked bridleway on the left and entering the Spa Ponds Nature Reserve. Follow the waymarked woodland path down to the ponds. The nature reserve was established in 1984 and is managed under licence by the Nottinghamshire Wildlife Trust. There are three medieval – probably 14th century – ponds, and one modern one, nestling in the woodland. The River Maun runs close by the site, and mining subsidence has caused the development of a swamp area, now planted with willows. There is an abundance of wildlife to look out for here, with aquatic plants and animals, and many varieties of dragonfly.

4. Cross the River Maun and continue, turning right at a crossways to follow a good track with wide forest views over the Maun valley to your right. Turn right with the track, descending to the valley. Turning left again beside the woods to continue along the track between the river on your right and a series of scenic fishing pools on the left.

5. Keep with this track, ignoring a bridge on the right, until the way turns sharp left at the end of the fish-pools. Leave the main track here, turning right, into the woods, on an ascending track. Where the track branches, take the left fork. Cross straight over an intersecting track and continue on a woodland footpath. Turn left on reaching a lane. Then turn right again by Cavendish Lodge, following Squires Lane through to Old Clipstone and the B6030. Left here, back to the Dog and Duck.

PLACES OF INTEREST

Sherwood Forest Farm Park, Lamb Pens Farm (GR 588653) is an approved centre for the rearing and preservation of many varieties of livestock, all of which can be seen by visitors. There are three small lakes, with a large collection of domestic and wild fowl. Additional attractions include a children's play area, gift shop and tea rooms. Open daily from April to October, 10.30 am to 5.15 pm. Charge payable. Telephone: 01623 823558.

THE HEART OF SHERWOOD

A walk in the very heart of the original, authentic and only Sherwood Forest. This combination of woodland and waterside takes you through the beautiful countryside forever associated with our legendary hero, Robin Hood.

The Major Oak.

Edwinstowe lies at the heart of Birklands (the birch lands), one of the best surviving areas of the ancient forest of Sherwood. It was here, in the parish church, that Robin and Marion were, according to tradition, united in marriage. A rather less reliable tradition is the one that maintains the outlaw band camped around – or even within – the Major Oak. Edwinstowe takes its name from King Edwin of Northumbria, who died in battle in AD 632 and whose body is believed to have lain on ground where the parish church now stands, and around which the village developed. The church (St Mary) dates from the 12th century, and Dr Brewer (he of the *Dictionary of Phrase and Fable*) is buried in the churchyard. At the time of the Domesday survey, the population of

Edwinstowe was recorded as about 20; rather fewer than that of today, which was swelled considerably by the development of the local colliery. Much of Birklands, including all the area around the Major Oak, is now dedicated as a country park, with an abundance of pleasant paths and tracks through the woodlands of birch, oak and pine. There is something for everyone here, with visitor information, exhibitions and video presentation, an activity centre, open air theatre, first aid point – and, of course, refreshment and toilet facilities – all within the bounds of the compact visitor centre. The River Maun is outside the area of the Country Park, but it, too, is indelibly linked to the Robin Hood stories. It is here, we are told, that Robin first met Little John in 'mortal combat', as a result of which Robin received a ducking!

The Forest Table – the Country Park's own refreshment facility – is strongly recommended for food and drink either before or after your walk. The atmosphere here is clean and pleasant, with smart, friendly service, and a varied menu at reasonable family prices. There is a selection of hot snacks, including quiche, chicken and mushroom pie, turkeyburger and vegetable pasty, and haddock and chips. Or you might try the all day breakfast, a Sherwood cream tea, or just a sandwich. And the under-twelves will just love a Chicken Teddy with chips, peas and a chocolate chip piggy!

Telephone: 01623 823202 or 01623 824490.

- **HOW TO GET THERE:** From the Ollerton roundabout, on the A614 trunk road, take the A6075 Mansfield road, turning right after about 2 miles (by Edwinstowe church) onto the B6034. The visitor centre car park is about ½ mile on from here.

  Stagecoach (East Midlands) operate an hourly bus service (Route 10/10a) in the week to Edwinstowe. This extends on Sunday (Routes 110/113) to serve the visitor centre.
- **PARKING:** There is ample parking available at the visitor centre, for which a small charge is levied.
- **LENGTH OF THE WALK:** 5 miles. Maps: OS Landranger 120 Mansfield and Worksop, OS Explorer 28 Sherwood Forest (GR 627676).

THE WALK

1. Leaving the Visitor Centre, first follow the waymarked route to reach the Major Oak. This great tree is believed by many to be the 'Greenwood Tree' beneath which Robin Hood and his Merry Men foregathered. I am sorry to disappoint you. 'Under the greenwood tree'

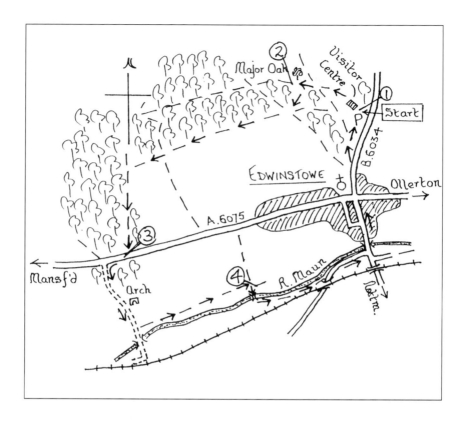

is, more likely, a general term meaning 'in the forest'. As for the tree itself, it is just possible that it was standing in Robin Hood's day. When I came here some years ago, I gathered that it was no more than 500 years old. Today, the adjacent information board says 800 years. Even so, it could never have been big enough, or significant enough, in Robin Hood's day to merit the outlaw's attention. The tree takes its name from one Major Rooke who, about 200 years ago, identified it as one of the mightiest oaks in the land.

2. Turn left opposite the Major Oak, following the directional waymark for Edwinstowe village and the fairground. On reaching a crossways turn right, immediately branching left and following a woodland path parallel with the edge of the woods. This is a fine, pleasant walk on a broad track through broad-leaved trees, largely oaks, typical of the true, ancient Sherwood Forest. Keep to the waymarked bridleway route, turning left eventually on reaching a broad intersecting ride, with pine woods now on your right. Continue to reach the A6075 road.

3. Turn right, keeping to the verge on the right of this fast road. Where a break appears on the left, cross over carefully and take the waymarked bridleway route, keeping to the clear trackway. Pass the Duke's Archway – a folly built by the Duke of Portland in 1842 – and continue down the hill to the River Maun. Turn left by the bridge, following the riverside path, keeping to the right as the river meanders below wooded heights of birch and bracken. The path then emerges onto open fields to continue straight ahead for a while.

4. Turn right at a junction, ignoring an immediate guide post against the flood dike, to rejoin the Maun, crossed by a footbridge. The path continues above the river to emerge onto a minor road on the edge of Lidgett – a suburb of Edwinstowe. Turn left and follow the road (Mill Lane) to its junction with the B6034. Turn left now and continue, through Edwinstowe, back to the Visitor Centre.

PLACES OF INTEREST

Rufford Country Park has acres of park and woodland, at the heart of which are the remains of a 12th century Cistercian Abbey. There is a lake, around which is a popular footpath, and which is home to many species of wildfowl. The Stable Block houses a craft shop and gallery, and there are excellent refreshment facilities, souvenir shop and formal gardens. Admission is free; for opening hours telephone 01623 824153.

MEDEN VALE

The Meden - twin to the Maun - is a shy little river, that accompanies you out from Market Warsop into green pastures and glorious woodland trails. There are reminders on this lovely walk, too, of the industrial past.

Gleadthorpe Lodge

Little remains today of Nottinghamshire's mining heritage. One or two struggling pits still survive, and the odd opencast site raises a few hackles. But apart from these, only a redundant mineral railway line or two and, here and there, the villages and townships that grew up around the collieries, serve to remind us of a once flourishing industry. The Meden Vale community used to be called Welbeck Colliery Village, until somebody decided that this title was, perhaps, too prosaic. And who would argue? Much as we may deplore the passing of the collieries no one, surely, would deny that the present name, reflecting the presence of the River Meden - twin to the Maun - is more appealing. Whatever the present status of the town - and of its near neighbour,

Market Warsop, a busy little town – nobody is likely to mistake its industrial origins. Once outside these urban confines, however, one is in a totally different environment of green fields and glorious woodland tracks.

The Hare and Hounds is a friendly and welcoming Kimberley house, situated in the very centre of Market Warsop town. Food is available every day from 11 am to 2.30 pm (12 till 2 pm on Sunday), with Chef's Specialities, Dish of the Day and Monster Breakfast particular favourites. There is a special Junior Menu for the kiddies – and the more mature patrons (ie, Senior Citizens) can, if they come between noon and 1.30 pm on Tuesday, enjoy a full three-course meal at a reduced price. The inn has a family room and an outside drinking area, and dogs are welcome. There is also a rumour (one reported sighting) of a red-headed ghost – believed to have been the daughter of an earlier licensee. You may park here (if using the facilities) while completing the walk, but be sure to ask permission – or you may find, when you return, that you have been clamped!

Telephone: 01623 842440.

- **HOW TO GET THERE:** The walk starts from Market Warsop, which sits astride the A60 Mansfield to Worksop road. If travelling via the A614 (Nottingham-Doncaster road), turn off west at Ollerton roundabout, following the A6075 through Edwinstowe and transferring onto the B6035.

  Warsop is well-served with regular bus services (Stagecoach East Midlands) from Mansfield, Worksop and Edwinstowe. Also (but not Sunday), from Leicester, Nottingham and Doncaster.
- **PARKING:** Parking is not easy in Warsop town centre, and you are recommended to use Burns Lane, in the vicinity of the Sports Centre (follow the road signs).
- **LENGTH OF THE WALK:** 6½ miles. Maps: OS Landranger 120 Mansfield and Worksop, OS Explorer 28 Sherwood Forest (GR 570683).

THE WALK

1. Follow Burns Lane away from the town and into open country. The River Meden is on the left here as you proceed, but it is a very secretive little river, and you will be lucky to gain even a glimpse of it through the woodland. More eye-catching are the wild flowers, with honeysuckle and wild roses in the summer hedgerows. Pass Burns Farm, keeping straight on ahead at a junction of ways, following the

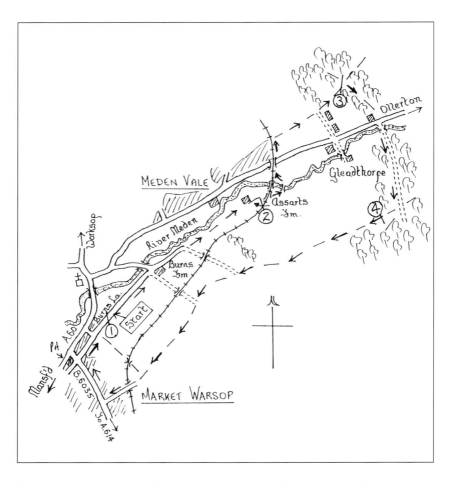

bridleway guidepost for Assarts Farm. Follow the track right and left past the farm buildings, continuing via the field track to pass beneath the mineral railway bridge, which used to carry coal from the local pit.

2. Keeping on over the field, turn left at a footpath waymark, to cross the Meden via a stout footbridge. Continue left around the field edge, initially with the river on your left. Cross a 'tall' stile, and on to the road, beside the railway bridge. Cross the road, continuing along the clear track beside the railway. More wild flowers here, in summer, with white campion prolific. At the head of the track, turn right, following the guide post as for Carburton. Keep straight forward at the next guidepost, and on to a third, at Gleadthorpe Plantation.

3. Turn right now, following a clear path through the wood to the road, by Gleadthorpe Lodge. Cross straight over and continue on the metalled driveway, crossing the river and climbing gently, still through fine woodland, to a crossways.

4. Turn right, and having done so keep straight forward, ignoring a more prominent track which bends left. Pass a guidepost and continue through the woods, with Gleadthorpe Grange below on your right. As the track leaves the woods, continue ahead over the fields. After passing a sewage works, ignore a right turn in the track and continue on the waymarked field path, bearing right a little over the fields. On reaching a lane, cross straight over and continue ahead along Upper Cross Lane, following a green track through to the outskirts of Market Warsop. Follow Cherry Grove down to the B6035 and turn right, back to Burns Lane.

PLACES OF INTEREST

Whaley Thorns Heritage Centre at Cockshut Lane, Whaley Thorns, Langwith is some distance from Warsop, but worth the diversion. Extensive displays of farm equipment and a re-creation of a Victorian coal-mine, in this former Edwardian infants school on the Derbyshire border. Guided tours of the centre, and guided walks in the surrounding countryside can be arranged, by phoning 01623 742525. Open all year, Sunday to Friday, 10 am to 4.30 pm. Admission free.

CRESWELL CRAGS

This is a gentle little walk through one of Britain's most fascinating sites. The stunningly beautiful, historically significant gorge of Creswell Crags, with its deep and lovely pond, lies right on the county boundary with Derbyshire. Here, in the distant days of the Ice Age, mammoth, woolly rhinoceros, reindeer – and man, the hunter gatherer – roamed.

Crags Pond

More than 10,000 years ago, our ancestors found shelter in the limestone caves of Creswell Crags. The surroundings were host to animal species, unknown in modern-day Britain, such as reindeer, bison and hyenas, and some, such as mammoth and woolly rhinoceros, which are now extinct. Today, perhaps, this area generally is better known in its triple role as an element in the Nottinghamshire/ Derbyshire coalfield, Sherwood Forest and the Dukeries. The crags, in fact, form a part of the Welbeck Estates, the seat of the Dukes of Portland, and the Dukeries Garden Centre, from where the walk commences, lies within the Welbeck Abbey grounds. Holbeck village is one of the four villages on the estate and the little churchyard contains many of the family graves.

No refreshments are available at Creswell Crags, other than ice creams and soft drinks. However, a feature of the Dukeries Garden Centre is the Welbeck Restaurant and Coffee Shop, which carries the Egon Ronay recommendation. You can sample anything from freshly percolated coffee or afternoon tea to a delicious three-course lunch, and everything is home-cooked from fresh local produce. There are non-smoking areas and outdoor picnic tables, and the car park is available for those patrons wishing to complete the walk (but do ensure that you return to your vehicle before closing time – or you may find the exit closed!).

Telephone: 01909 476506.

- **HOW TO GET THERE:** The Dukeries Garden Centre is on the eastern side of the A60 road, approximately mid-way between Cuckney and Worksop. If wishing to park at the Creswell Crags Visitor Centre, access is via the B6042, just over ½ mile north of the garden centre.

  Stagecoach East Midlands (route 32: Mansfield-Cuckney-Worksop) passes Welbeck Abbey gates, seven journeys daily, including Sunday. A jointly operated hourly bus service (Route 757: Stagecoach/Barton's: Leicester-Nottingham-Mansfield-Worksop-Doncaster), also passes the gates, Monday to Saturday.

- **PARKING:** As indicated above, you may park at the Garden Centre if using their facilities. Parking is also available at the Creswell Crags Visitor Centre (as an alternative starting point for the walk).

- **LENGTH OF THE WALK:** 3 miles. Maps: OS Landranger 120 Mansfield and Worksop, OS Explorer 28 Sherwood Forest (GR 548741).

THE WALK

1. Starting from the Dukeries Garden Centre car park, turn right outside the gates, following the A60 north for about ¼ mile. Turn left beside a lodge, taking the waymarked bridleway route along a wooded track for a further ½ mile, to arrive at the Creswell Crags Visitor Centre. No visit to Creswell Crags would be complete without calling in at the Visitor Centre for an enthralling exposition of the discoveries made here over the last century and a half, revealing a most vivid picture of life as it was here 10,000 years ago.

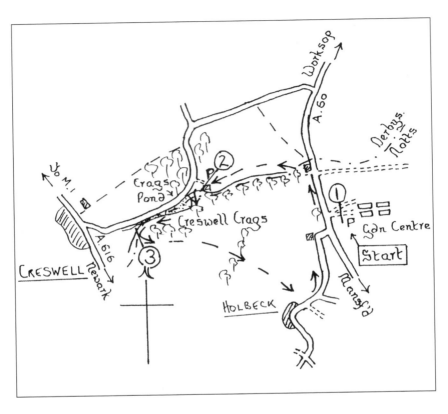

2. From the Visitor Centre, follow the footpath leading to the crags. This brings you to the foot of Crags Pond, an attractive feature of the gorge (and, of course, the 'waterside' of our walk). The pond is not an entirely natural feature, having been created over a century ago for the specific purpose of duck shooting. Happily, the mallard we see here today enjoy a much safer, happier existence. And the pond – of quite substantial dimensions – does fit nicely into the landscape of the gorge, flanked as it is on either side by impressive limestone crags.

Follow the path round to the left of the pond, with the crags on your left, passing the Boathouse Cave. This is the first of a number of caves in the face of the crags which were used in the past by early man, and inside which the remains of them and their diet and artefacts have been unearthed. It is not possible, in the ordinary way, to enter the caves, although conducted tours are possible at times under supervision. It is possible to continue right round the gorge, returning via the opposite

Creswell Crags

bank of the pond to the Visitor Centre. If doing so, you will need to retrace your steps to the head of the gorge to continue this walk.

3. Beyond the Church Hole Cave, the head of the gorge is reached, with a footpath leading off left. Follow this steeply round up the hillside as waymarked, branching left at a post, to reach and cross a stile beside a wood. Continue ahead over the fields, bearing off a little from the wood to reach another stile. Beyond this the way maintains a straight line, mainly beside the hedges, to reach the road at the village of Holbeck. Turn left and follow the road round to its junction with the A60. Then left again, back to the garden centre.

PLACES OF INTEREST

The Harley Gallery at Welbeck, Worksop, supports a community of craftsmen and women, selected for their high standards of skill and workmanship. Skills include tapestry weaving, organ building and bowmaking, and a complementary programme of exhibitions, concerts and lectures is scheduled throughout the year. Open Easter to October; 11.30 am to 5 pm, Thursday to Sunday and Bank Holiday Mondays. Telephone: 01909 501700.

CLUMBER PARK AND LAKE
❧❀❧

A delightful stroll in the heart of Sherwood Forest, offering a pleasant blend of mixed woodland, open parkland at Clumber, and a beautiful 'ducal' lake.

Clumber Park Lake

One of Nottinghamshire's primary tourist areas – largely synonymous with Sherwood Forest – is the Dukeries, a vast area of woodland and parkland containing the three ducal estates of Welbeck, Thoresby and Clumber. All of these estates have 'fallen from Their Graces', but Clumber lives on as the regional headquarters of the National Trust, and the park has taken on a new lease of life as a popular Country Park. Until the late 18th century, when the Duke of Newcastle built the house, Clumber is said to have been a barren waste, inhabited only by rabbits. It is a situation difficult to envisage as you explore the parkland today, a particularly delightful feature of which is the lake, adapted from a dammed section of the River Poulter. The Park is open all year, during daylight hours. Admission is free, although those wishing to drive onto the estate (other than National Trust members) will be required to pay a parking fee. Certain facilities, including the walled gardens, vineries etc, are open only on a seasonal basis, and a small fee may be required for these also. Fuller details can be obtained by telephoning 01909 476592.

There is a self-service cafeteria within the estate, offering a selection of light snacks. There is also a restaurant with waitress service, and here it is possible to obtain a full à la carte meal. These facilities are open daily throughout the year with the exception of Christmas Day and Boxing Day, and advance restaurant bookings are accepted. Telephone: 01909 484122.

- **HOW TO GET THERE:** The walk begins outside the Clumber Estate, and the main entrance (on the A614 Nottingham to Doncaster road) is not used. To reach the free public parking area, turn off the A57 road, about 1 mile west of the A1 roundabout. Or leave the B6034 (Worksop to Budby) road, turning east, 1 mile south of the A57. The parking area is on the north side of this unclassified road, east of the bend by Truman's Lodge.

  Unfortunately, no reliable bus services have been identified.
- **PARKING:** At the Forest Cottage Plantation as above.
- **LENGTH OF THE WALK:** 6 miles. Maps: OS Landranger 120 Mansfield and Worksop, OS Explorer 28 Sherwood Forest (GR 619762).

THE WALK

1. Leaving the parking area, cross the road and enter the woodland. Turn left almost immediately, following a track running parallel to the road, to meet a broad bridleway and turn right. Continue through the woods, alternating between conifers and broadleaves. Cross an open space (the Barbecue Site), and reach Limetree Avenue. Turn left along the road a little way; then right again at a guidepost, rejoining the bridleway.

2. Where the path branches, break left through the pines as directed by the 'Bridleway' arrow-mark, crossing a minor road and continuing, now through broadleaves, to the next road. Turn right.

Follow this road almost to Hardwick village. Go right again at a junction, bypassing the village and reaching the eastern arm of the lake. A well-trodden path now leads to the River Poulter, crossed by means of a footbridge at the lake-foot. A superb walk follows, along the

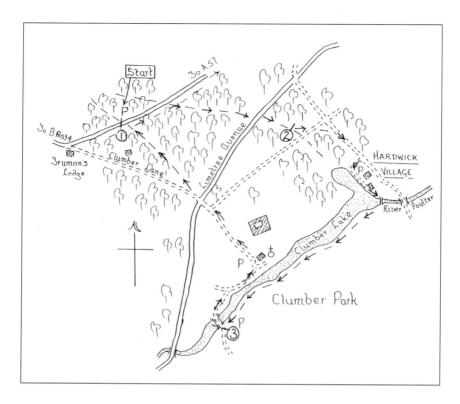

southern edge of the lake, with splendid views across to Clumber church and administrative buildings. But beware of bikes as you walk, which, in these progressive days, no longer seem to be provided with any form of warning device! The church of St Mary the Virgin was commissioned by the 7th Duke of Newcastle, and was dedicated in 1889. The stonework is white with red dressings, and there is a red crossing tower with a darker spire. It has elaborate woodcarving within.

3. Cross Clumber Bridge, which is in classical style in the spirit of its surroundings, and turn back along the lakeside to reach a road which is followed to the visitor facilities. The administrative buildings are outbuildings of the former Clumber House (most of the house has been demolished, only the Duke's study surviving). They include the National Trust Regional Offices, but the visitor facilities – shop, cafe/restaurant, toilets etc – are also here. Elsewhere there is a walled

A popular spot in Clumber Park

garden, vineries, and an exhibition of garden tools. Having satisifed your needs, leave the buildings complex, rejoining the road and following the wall away from the lake. Bear left at a junction and continue, passing the cricket field and the entrance kiosk, to reach Limetree Avenue. Cross the avenue, then bear right at the bridleway (Robin Hood Way) guidepost, and continue ahead, back to the road and parking area.

PLACES OF INTEREST
Mr Straw's House at 7 Blyth Grove, Worksop, a National Trust property, is a semi-detached house built at the turn of the century, and a time-capsule of a 1920s lifestyle. Open Tuesday to Saturday, end of March to end of October, 11 am to 5 pm; last admission 4 pm. Admission is by prior booking, timed ticket only, by calling 01909 482380 (National Trust members free).

TO WHITSUNDAY PIE LOCK

After a challenging first half-mile, the going on this enjoyable walk becomes easy, with a high-level green lane offering distant views across the open plain. The return journey follows a pleasant section of the Chesterfield Canal.

Whitsunday Pie Lock

The Chesterfield Canal, the first to be built in Nottinghamshire, crosses the county from west of Worksop to its outflow at West Stockwith. It was opened in 1772 The total length, from Chesterfield to West Stockwith, was 46 miles, incorporating 65 locks and two tunnels. The route was surveyed by James Brindley, but most of the work was carried out under the supervision of his deputy, John Varley. The Chesterfield end of the canal has been cut off for many years, following the collapse, in 1908, of Norwood Tunnel, but most, if not all, of the Nottinghamshire stretch is still open and in use. There are some delightful stretches to be enjoyed by the walker and the angler, and by the waterborne traveller. After passing through Retford, the canal turns north, running in fairly close communion with the River Idle, with a level plain on the one side counterbalanced by higher ground on the other and passing the twin villages of Clarborough and Hayton.

The Gate, on Smeath Lane, Clarborough, is an attractive canalside free house offering friendly service and excellent food and drink, and popular both with walkers and with anglers. The main part of the house dates back 270 years – pre-dating the canal itself – and the tasteful blend of old beams and half-timbering with attractive brassware and a cheerful coal-fire serve to emphasise the traditional atmosphere. A more modern, purpose-built restaurant overlooks the canal. Lunchtime opening is from 11.30 am to 2.30 pm in the week, and 12 noon until 3 pm on Sunday. Opening time in the evening varies between 5.30 pm and 6.30 pm; and 7 pm on Sunday. Food is available daily; lunchtime from noon until 2 pm (2.30 pm on Sunday) and in the evening until 9.30 pm. The speciality of the house (appropriate to the location, but not an indication of the source!) is the full fish menu. Bar snacks and sandwiches are also available, at lunch times only. Real ales include Adnams and Evolution Ale (from Darwin Brewery in County Durham).

Telephone: 01777 703397.

- **HOW TO GET THERE:** The walk starts from the A620 (Gainsborough road) at Welham, just outside Retford. Turn off against the Hop Pole Inn onto a now-redundant section of roadway with ample space for parking.

  A regular daily bus service (Roadcar) operates between Retford and Gainsborough.
- **PARKING:** Off the A620 at Welham, as above.
- **LENGTH OF THE WALK:** 4½ miles. Maps: OS Landranger 120 Mansfield and Worksop, OS Pathfinder 745 East Retford and Blyth (GR 720819).

THE WALK

1. The first ½ mile of this walk follows a neglected and overgrown footpath, a little difficult in places and crossing an active rail line. If you are feeling less adventurous, or have a wheelchair or baby buggy with you, this section may be omitted in favour of the main road (with its traffic – but there is a pavement), as far as the road junction at Little Gringley Lane/Pinfold Lane. In that case start following the directions again at 2 below.

Starting from the lay-by, a footpath – not waymarked – leaves the

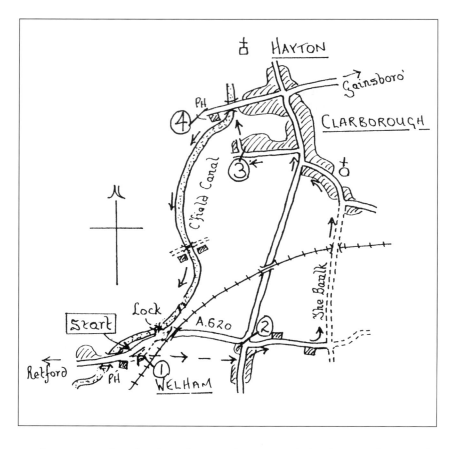

roadway on a bend, via a barrier bar. Bear left along a faint path, crossing a footway over a stream and continuing, with the hedge on your left, to a stile and the railway line. This line is in regular use, so cross with great care. Across the line, the way continues along 'Shady Lane'. The title is misleading, because the 'lane' is now no more than a footpath, and a somewhat difficult one at that, with a ditch alongside and seriously overgrown. But it is passable, with care – and adds a little extra spice to the walk! After about ½ mile, the path emerges onto Little Gringley Lane. Turn left here and follow the road down to the A620, turning sharp right on the junction to follow Pinfold Lane.

2. Continue, climbing gently, to a crossways and turn left, now following The Baulk; a splendid high-level green lane, with distant views over the plain to the west. Follow The Baulk through to Clarborough, joining the metalled road and continuing round left, to reach the A620. Turn right; then left again at Big Lane.

3. At the top of Big Lane, turn right along Broad Gores, continuing over the succeeding field path, and bearing left where the path forks, to a recreational area. Cross the stile and follow the metalled footpath to Smeath Lane, crossing the canal bridge to reach the Gate Inn.

4. Join the towpath, following the canal south. This is a lovely, relaxing path, not heavily used, with verdant banks and a plentiful supply of anglers and wildfowl. The canal is left at 'Whitsunday Pie Lock' – a delightful name – via Bridge no 60. Join the road, crossing straight over to join the footpath and turn right, back to the lay-by.

PLACES OF INTEREST
Bassetlaw Museum, Amcott House, 40 Grove Street, Retford. There is a wide variety of enthralling exhibits to be seen in this modern conversion of a fine old 18th century house. These include 18/19th century glassware, pottery and porcelain, saltglaze stoneware jugs, agricultural and household implements and utensils, and archaeological finds dating back to Roman times and the Bronze Age. Open daily, except Sunday and Bank Holidays. Telephone: 01777 706741.

THE CHESTERFIELD CANAL AT CLAYWORTH

Short and sweet, this one, with lots of narrow boats resting at their moorings on one of the county's most attractive, navigable stretches of canal, followed by a gentle stroll along a quiet, village street.

The Chesterfield Canal.

In the quiet north of the county, the village of Clayworth stands astride the Roman road between Doncaster and Lincoln; unclassified here, as befits a peaceful, unspoilt village with few concessions to 20th century fancies. The tower of Clayworth parish church has some base-work dating back to the 12th century or earlier. The upper part, which has been rebuilt, has eight fine pinnacles and eight gargoyles. Other parts of the church were added or rebuilt in later periods; the nave in the 13th and the clerestory in the 15th century. There is also some fine, more modern work, in the stained glass of the gallery. Memorials in the church include those to two brothers of the Otter family (of Roystone

Manor, Clayworth), one of whom was killed at Flanders, and the other in an accident. There are also two excellent pubs in the village, and the headquarters of the Retford and Worksop Boat Club. The Chesterfield Canal winds tidily round the village on the south-western side, neatly avoiding the village itself but remaining close enough to serve as a valuable local amenity.

The Blacksmiths Arms, on Town Street, is a cheerful and welcoming house providing excellent food and drink seven days a week, lunchtime and evening. There is a comprehensive bar menu of full meals and snacks, including grills, sandwiches and ploughman's lunches. A special children's menu also. If you wish for a meal with more style, the associated Wiseton Restaurant offers both table d'hote and à la carte selections, as well as being available for private functions. Telephone: 01777 818171.

Also on Town Street, the Brewers Arms is open lunchtime (except Monday) and evening, food being available from Tuesday to Sunday. Telephone: 01777 816107.

- **HOW TO GET THERE:** Clayworth is reached via the B1403, from either Gringley on the Hill on the A631 Doncaster to Gainsborough road, or Hayton on the A620 Retford to Gainsborough road.

   Roadcar Services 96/97 (Retford, Misterton, Gainsborough) serve Clayworth with an hourly bus service from Monday to Saturday.
- **PARKING:** There is ample roadside parking space available in Clayworth itself, but the most convenient spot for the purpose of the walk is just outside the village, on the verge by Clayworth Bridge (the Hayton road).
- **LENGTH OF THE WALK:** 2 miles. This walk can safely be undertaken by (accompanied) wheelchair users. Maps: OS Landranger 120 Mansfield and Worksop, OS Pathfinder 745 East Retford and Blyth (GR 732877).

THE WALK

1. Starting from Clayworth Bridge (on the Hayton road), join the canal towpath. Before commencing the walk proper, you are recommended to turn right under the bridge, following the paved path along the wharf past the Boat Club buildings. Enjoy the colourful array of narrow boats and launches moored alongside, with a smattering of waterfowl besporting themselves in and around the canal. Return to the bridge, continuing now along the towpath in a south-westerly direction. After passing the last of the moorings, the hard track reverts to an unsurfaced

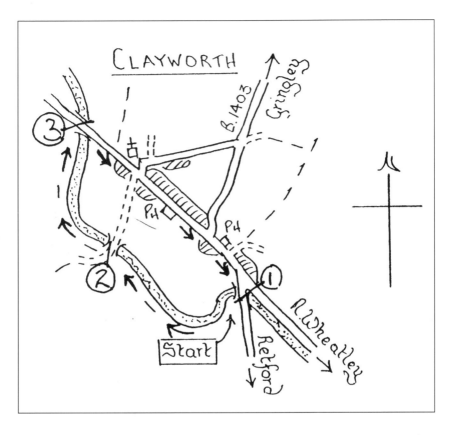

path. Some care is needed here at first, as there is an awkward camber to the path, but this soon gives way to a broad grass track which persists for the rest of the canal-side walk.

2. Pass beneath Otter's Bridge (named, apparently, after the Otter family who used to reside in the nearby Elizabethan Royston Manor – not, sadly, the water-mammals of the same name!). Continue as far as Gray's Bridge, joining the road here and turning right.

3. Keep on along Wiseton Road, into Clayworth village, passing St Peter's church. Then on along Town Street, bearing right at the Wheatley Road junction, over Clayworth Bridge and back to your starting point.

Otter's Bridge, Clayworth.

PLACES OF INTEREST

Mattersey Priory ruins (GR: SK 703896) are situated on the bank of the River Idle, at the end of a rough track to the east of Mattersey village. The site of a Gilbertine priory, this was the only house of the order in Nottinghamshire. It was never a wealthy house. In the early 12th century days there were only six canons and, though the numbers fluctuated over the years, there were only five surviving at the dissolution in 1528. In the parish church at Mattersey, there are two stone reliefs which probably came from the priory. Open daily (English Heritage). No telephone contact number.

THE MEETING OF THE WATERS, WEST STOCKWITH

In the course of its journey north through Nottinghamshire, the Trent has absorbed a host of lesser rivers, streams and canals. Here at West Stockwith, just a mile or so from the point where the Trent finally leaves us for South Humberside and the sea, she takes in the Chesterfield Canal and the River Idle. This excellent little walk from West Stockwith visits all three waterways.

West Stockwith

The little Trentside village of West Stockwith is another of those settlements which, although securely anchored in Nottinghamshire, probably has a greater affinity with Lincolnshire. Its twin, East Stockwith, lies on the other side of the county boundary, which here follows the river, and Gainsborough, the nearest town of any size, is also in Lincolnshire. This is low-lying fen country, and the local waterways are popular with anglers and with boat-people, as well as providing excellent easy walking along the towpaths and flood-banks. West Stockwith was an inland port and a centre for boat building, long before the advent of the canal. One local man, William Huntingdon, made sufficient from his work as a ship's carpenter to found several charities and build the little church. His monument, within the building, depicts Huntingdon reclining on one elbow and displaying, in his other hand, the plan of a sailing ship. Nowadays, there are no commercial craft to be seen at Stockwith – but plenty of pleasure boats along the canal, and in the marina.

The walk begins and ends at the Waterfront Inn, on Canal Lane, West Stockwith. A clean and friendly free house, it is in a perfect situation directly alongside the Chesterfield Canal and opposite the West Stockwith Marina and Lock, where the canal empties into the Trent. Real ales include John Smith's, Marston's Pedigree, Charlie Wells Bombardier and Shepherd Neame Spitfire, with a guest ale at the weekends. Meals and bar snacks are served lunchtimes and evenings, daily and a comprehensive menu, displayed on the board in the lounge bar, includes the usual range of steaks and fish dishes, pies, ploughman's lunches and jacket potatoes. There is also a splendid variety of sandwiches for those with simpler tastes. Families with well-behaved children are welcome, and there is an outside drinking and children's play area.

Telephone: 01427 891223.

Also on the route of the walk, the Packet Inn at Misterton (telephone: 01427 890559) and the White Hart at West Stockwith (telephone: 01427 890176) both offer alternative eating and drinking opportunities.

- **HOW TO GET THERE:** From the A631 (Bawtry to Gainsborough) road at Beckingham, follow the A161 as far as Misterton, turning right here for West Stockwith.

  There are regular daily bus services (Roadcar) between Retford, Misterton and Gainsborough, and (except Sunday) between Lincoln, Gainsborough and Doncaster, all of which visit West Stockwith.
- **PARKING:** Genuine patrons may park at the Waterfront Inn – but verbal confirmation is advised. Those not visiting the pub should be able to find adequate roadside parking space in the vicinity.
- **LENGTH OF THE WALK:** 2½ miles. Maps: OS Landranger 112 Scunthorpe, OS Pathfinder 728 Harworth and Gringley (GR 789947).

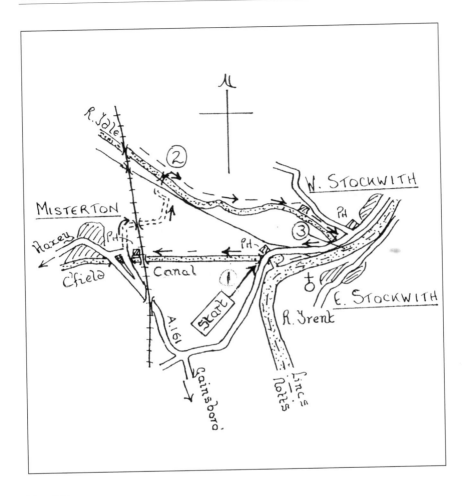

THE WALK

1. Join the canal at Basin Bridge, following the towpath to Misterton, passing beneath the railway and joining the road at the Packet Inn. Misterton developed largely as a result of the draining of the Isle of Axholme marshes, which produced excellent arable land, thus bringing employment and agriculture, to the area. Some of the local farms date back to the early 17th century, mingling with Victorian and Georgian architecture. The opening of the Chesterfield Canal brought further prosperity to the village, partly through its commercial value but also, as a 'fallout' from its construction through the development of a thriving brick industry.

The pub at the start of the walk.

Turning right onto Soss Lane, follow this quiet lane out of the town, passing the Covertside Boarding Kennels. Continue round to the left with the track to reach and cross the River Idle.

2. Turn right again, downstream, following the track along the top of the floodbank. After passing the waterworks buildings, bear right, rejoining the floodbank and continuing to the road at West Stockwith. Do not be put off by the fact that the footpath appears to pass through the grounds of a private house – you will find, when you reach the road, that it is waymarked!

3. Cross the road and turn right, looking out for a run of steps on your left. Follow these on to the River Trent floodbank and continue to West Stockwith Marina and Lock. Cross the lock gates and follow the road round to the steps, and Basin Bridge.

And now, having swallowed up all her Nottinghamshire tributaries, the Trent leaves our county, bound for the Humber estuary and the North Sea. But rivers, unlike man, are constant. And, even as the tidal flow leaves us far behind, the Soar and the Erewash, 70 miles to the south, continue their eternal task of feeding our premier waterway.

INFORMATION

Tourist Information Centres covering the area include:

Mansfield: Old Town Hall, Market Place. Tel: 01623 427770
Newark: Gilstrap Centre, Castlegate. Tel: 01636 78962
Nottingham: 1-4, Smithy Row. Tel: 0115 947 0661
Ollerton: Sherwood Heath. Tel: 01623 824545
Retford: Amcott House, Grove Street. Tel: 01777 860780
West Bridgford: County Hall, Loughborough Road. Tel: 0115 977 3558
Worksop: Public Library, Memorial Avenue. Tel: 01909 501148

Bus Hotlines

Nottingham. Tel: 0115 924 0000
Retford. Tel: 01777 710550

Rail Enquiries

Times and Fares; all national services Tel: 0345 48 49 50